Educational Upward Mobility

Also by Antonia Kupfer

UNIVERSITÄT UND SOZIALE GERECHTIGKEIT: Eine Bilanz der Hochschulreformen seit 1998 (*2004*)

DOKTORANDINNEN IN DEN USA: Eine Analyse vor dem Hintergrund des Bologna – Prozesses (*2007*)

GLOBALISATION, HIGHER EDUCATION, THE LABOUR MARKET AND INEQUALITY (*editor, 2012*)

PROMOVIEREN IN EUROPA. Ein internationaler Vergleich von Promotionsbedingungen (*with J. Moes, 2004*)

Educational Upward Mobility

Practices of Social Changes

Antonia Kupfer

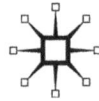
First published 2015 by
PALGRAVE MACMILLAN

Palgrave Macmillan in the UK is an imprint of Macmillan Publishers Limited, registered in England, company number 785998, of Houndmills, Basingstoke, Hampshire RG21 6XS.

Palgrave Macmillan in the US is a division of St Martin's Press LLC, 175 Fifth Avenue, New York, NY 10010.

Palgrave Macmillan is the global academic imprint of the above companies and has companies and representatives throug hout the world.

Palgrave® and Macmillan® are registered trademarks in the United States, the United Kingdom, Europe and other countries.

ISBN: 978–1–137–35530–0

This book is printed on paper suitable for recycling and made from fully managed and sustained forest sources. Logging, pulping and manufacturing processes are expected to conform to the environmental regulations of the country of origin.

A catalogue record for this book is available from the British Library.

A catalog record for this book is available from the Library of Congress.

To Donata Amara

Contents

List of Tables

Acknowledgments

Professor Emeritus Beate Krais accompanied the writing process of this book, prompting many fruitful discussions for which I am very grateful. Julie Edelson, PhD, corrected my English and sharpened my insights. Tony Crawford kindly revised all my translations of the Austrian interviews into English. To all: my sincere thanks!

Introduction

Educational upward mobility is not the American Dream plus IQ. It requires more than individual effort and intelligence, and sometimes completely different ingredients, such as specific social and societal conditions. It is still exceptional; most people from working-class families and lower socioeconomic backgrounds do not enter higher education. The topic is tricky because success depends on social structures, on the one hand, without being a mass phenomenon, on the other.

A large, important field of research has revealed the discrimination, barriers, and problems that impede working-class people from moving on to higher education and university degrees. Education is not neutral, but designed by and for middle-class people. Still, some succeed. Why? What enabled them to go where the vast majority of their counterparts do not? This book offers answers to these questions.

Chapter 1 begins by outlining the research field and analyzing the literature. It becomes clear that we know very little about the conditions that enable educational upward mobility, and empirical research on the question is thin. This book aims to fill the gap. By adducing empirical data to explore educational institutions, systems, and the relations between education and employment in two very different countries, Austria and England, a wide range of social contexts and societal conditions for educational upward mobility are illuminated.

To draw objective conclusions from these factors, a theoretical framework is needed. Chapter 2 explains why I decided to apply sociologist Pierre Bourdieu's fundamental view of societies as stratified and his concept of habitus. Habitus is a category that permits analysis of both structures and agency and how they are interrelated, mutually constitutive, and inseparable. Furthermore, it is an instrument for analyzing processes; it allows me to analyze social contexts and circumstances, such as modernization, and outline how social change takes place by demonstrating how working-class people perceive and address, for example, newly introduced participatory elements of the Catholic Church, in a way that contributes to social upward mobility.

Chapter 3 discusses methods. The empirical data of this study come from 18 biographical narrative interviews with educationally upwardly mobile people, 12 in Austria and six in England. Interviewees were born between 1928 and 1978, and interviews were conducted until summer 2012. Thus, the study covers almost a century of social, political, economic, and cultural development in two countries. To analyze the interviews, I combined Bourdieu's perspective on research practice with Gabriele Rosenthal's method of reconstructing life histories.

The largest part of the book, Chapter 4, demonstrates and evaluates the social circumstances enabling educational upward mobility that emerged from the interviews. The data show the impact of concrete social contexts and societal conditions on the educational upward mobility of working-class people in Austria and England. Their life histories demonstrate how social change actually takes place, how certain social structures create perceptions and logic that lead to certain actions and lifestyles that differ from those of their parents and move them from the working class toward the middle class. Note again that I am not proposing that whole cohorts of working-class students became socially upwardly mobile, but that exceptions took place *due to, and embedded in,* social and societal structures. The book ends with a summary of findings and conclusions.

1
Research Literature on Educational Upward Mobility

Educational upward mobility is a complex topic, so the following literature review on research in the field is rather elaborate. It starts by locating this book in the wider field of social mobility. It then groups studies on educational upward mobility, starting at the microsociological level of motives, proceeding to the meso level of educational institutions, and extending to the macro level of societal factors. Finally, studies with other approaches are considered.

1.1 Review of the field

The topic of educational upward mobility is part of the wider concept of vertical social mobility, which relies on a hierarchical society in which people generally obtain positions based on their income, the prestige of their occupation, and the level and prestige of their formal educational degrees. Social mobility comprises an individual perspective of moving up or down a social ladder and a societal perspective of changing gaps between social classes or social groups of similar economic backgrounds.

Surprisingly, few seem to question social mobility as such and its dependence on societal hierarchy (a recent exception is Reay, 2013). In place of recommending social upward mobility, no one proposes the concept of reducing social hierarchies as a way to increase social equality or improve underprivileged people's living conditions. Since this book focuses on educational upward mobility among working-class people, it does not present the literature on other important social inequalities, such as those related to gender and ethnicity. However, gender and ethnic inequalities are often intertwined with socioeconomic inequalities, and studies explicitly relating them are taken into consideration.

Social mobility studies generally reference education in terms of the degrees that define individuals' positions in societies, or its role is debated: does it support social mobility or maintain social hierarchies? This debate is tightly connected to the research area of social inequalities in education. Broadly speaking, findings of low social inequalities in education support education's contribution to social mobility and findings of large social inequalities refute education's contribution. In my view, research overwhelmingly reveals social inequalities in education. The literature ascribing reasons for the underrepresentation of working-class people in university degree programs is large. Findings based on rational choice models point to differences in class choices in the area of education due to different costs and benefits (Breen & Jonsson, 2005; Goldthorpe, 1996).

Studies related to Bourdieu's concepts of habitus, field, and capital reveal a variety of explanations. For example, class differences in access to information on good and bad schools lead to a classed selection of schools that reproduces social homogeneity in schools (Ball, 2003; Ball et al., 1997). However, equal information is not the solution, because the idea of choice assumes a kind of formal equality that obscures the effects of real inequalities (Ball et al., 2002). Choice in general is rooted in the discrimination and classification of places in a hierarchical order that leads working-class people to less prestigious (higher) education institutions (Reay et al., 2005). Such structures as the academic–vocational divide of institutions, curricula, and qualifications play a key role in reproducing inequalities, diverting working-class people onto lower-status vocational tracks (Becker & Hecken, 2008, 2009a, b). Education systems can also be seen as products of inequality, created by decision makers using organizational and institutional structures (Berger & Kahlert, 2005).

Issues of identity are crucial in educational processes, so a lack of positive images of working-class people contributes to their educational disqualification and inadequate academic support (Reay, 2001). Based on internalized images, working-class pupils do not opt for higher education because they expect to fail. Subtle practices in schools work to 'other' and exclude working-class teachers

(Maguire, 2005). Fees impede or deter some working-class people from studying, fearing large debts (Heine & Quast, 2011). In sum, research has revealed various sources and mechanisms that, individually and together, work to exclude working-class people from higher education.

However, this book focuses on the exception, educational upward mobility, so the following literature review does not include the rich research studies on social inequality in education (e.g., Ball, 2006; Boudon, 1974; Jencks, 1972; Kozlik, 1965; Müller & Karle, 1993; Reay et al., 2006), the debate on whether educational expansion reduced social inequalities in education (e.g., Blossfeld, 1993; Henz & Maas, 1995; Müller & Haun, 1994; Shavit et al., 2007), and the general debate on whether the role of education is to support or to impede social equality (Erikson & Jonsson, 1996).

1.2 Social upward mobility in relation to education

Research on social mobility can be categorized in various ways. Coxon and Jones (1975) grouped key texts partly chronologically and partly according to concepts and measurements of social mobility. Goldthorpe (1985) distinguished concepts of social mobility according to differences in the authors' normative and political interests. He identified two categories, one that operates within a framework of class structure and another that operates within a framework of social hierarchy or ranking, but this differentiation seems problematic, since a class structure *is* a social hierarchy. Groß (2008) identified 'three generations' of social mobility research since the Second World War that differ mainly in their methodological approaches. Weischer (2011) categorized the field by the investigators' geographical origins: for example, Anglo-American mobility research.

I would like to offer another approach that addresses the dimensions most crucial for generating social upward mobility. Three broad categories of factors can be identified: individual motives, educational systems, and societal structures. Broadly speaking, these distinctions follow the chronological development of scientific research on the subject as well as sociological levels of analysis, from micro to meso to macro. Since these levels are ideal categories, they are useful for defining the research focus, but social phenomena are not restricted to one level. My overview will *not* imply, for example, that studies on the individual motives crucial for upward mobility deal only with certain individuals' motives and not the related societal structures and social contexts.

1.2.1   Motives contributing to upward social mobility

The earliest studies considering the motives crucial for upward mobility started from the assumption of a culturally embedded, universal (although implicitly male) desire to ascend. Following Merton (1938), upward mobility in the United States materializes through individuals' internalization of the dominant ideology of social ascendency. He clearly linked the micro- and macrosociological levels: 'our egalitarian ideology denies by implication the existence of non competing groups and individuals in the pursuit of pecuniary success' (p. 680). His primary intention was to contribute to the research, not on social mobility, but on deviance or anomaly. In a society where the 'same body of success-symbols is held to be desirable for all' (p. 680), poverty is associated with crime more often than in more openly stratified societies, such as those in southeastern Europe. There, according to Merton, people tend to accept social hierarchies, so classes differ in their values and objectives. His observation that most (male) Americans internalize a normative idea of social ascent still seems to be a driving force for acquiring higher education today. Note that the widely shared value of social ascent attributed to US society was reflected among my interviewees in both Austria and Britain. As I will demonstrate in Chapter 4, interviewees expressed ascending aspirations as part of their socialization in working-class families. This value may have spread with other US values and cultural features in European countries after the Second World War.

Like Merton, McClelland (1961) held that social dimensions are crucial for the creation of motives, but he went a step further by distinguishing different motives based on different social contexts. As a psychologist, his main assertion was that economic development depends not only on socioeconomic factors, such as the relations of production, but also on psychological factors, such as motivation: 'The hypothesis that gave rise to the present study is that achievement motivation is in part responsible for economic growth' (p. 36). He aimed to explain performance differences by motivations arising from specific personality factors that, in turn, depend on the social context in which they were created. He analyzed the value systems and educational styles of families of different social classes to determine their influence on performance motivation. In addition, he followed Weber (1930), who identified the Protestant ethic as a major element of the attitudes and actions that drive capitalist economy. According to McClelland, Protestant education is partly responsible for high achievement, based on empirical data he collected on the variables 'mothers' attitudes', 'sons' values', 'entrepreneurial behaviour', and '*n* Achievement' in four countries. By '*n* Achievement', he refers specifically to the desire to do something better, faster, more efficiently, and with less effort. 'It is not a generalized desire to succeed, nor is it related to doing well at all sorts of enterprises. ... Rather it is peculiarly associated with moderate risk-taking because any task which allows one to choose the level of difficulty at which he works also permits him to figure out how to be more efficient at it, how to get the most benefit (utility) for the least cost' (1976, p. A).

McClelland's approach was restricted to measurable behavior. He assumed that motives are relatively general and stable features of personality, coined by early childhood experiences. He followed Winterbottom's results to conclude that 'early mastery training promotes high *n* Achievement, *provided* it does not reflect generalized restrictiveness, authoritarianism, or "rejection" by the parents' (1961, p. 345, emphasis original). In his introduction to the revised edition, he retracted his previous statement on the significance of childhood experiences for achievement, arguing that at the time he had 'accepted the Freudian notion that basic personality drives are laid down in early childhood', but now thought that *n* Achievement 'can be raised in short intensive training courses for adults' (1976, p. E).

McClelland's study contributes important insights on children's socialization and their development and later expression of certain attitudes, motives, and actions. His empirical data demonstrated that the neoclassical paradigm of rational action in the economy is not reflected in reality, but he did not answer questions about whether high achievement actually leads to a higher social position. To find out, we would have to analyze the social contexts in which social ascent takes place: high performance alone would determine social ascent only in a purely meritocratic society, which has never existed.

In societies where meritocratic values and practices compete with others – for example, distribution of jobs based on social capital – motivation, achievement, and its impacts would have to be analyzed in relation to social power structures. In addition, McClelland addressed only intentional and consciously evoked education, and missed unintentional and unconscious attitudes and actions. I will show that several of the people I interviewed demonstrated high achievement without aiming to perform well.

Goldthorpe and Lockwood (1963) proposed that people hold different understandings of mobility based on their social position. They discussed whether affluent workers undergo a process of *'embourgeoisement'*, aligning with middle-class people, or whether working- and middle-class alignment have independent causes. The former implies a normative shift: 'assimilation' of middle-class values 'through aspiration' of working-class members (p. 151), perhaps as part of the post-war Americanization process noted above. In contrast, an independent convergence would rely on the assumption that 'changes in economic institutions and in the conditions of urban life ... weakened simultaneously the "collectivism" of the [working class] and the "individualism" of the [middle class]' (p. 152). The authors dismissed both interpretations in their conclusion and stuck to a relatively clear-cut class difference, despite the phenomenon of affluent workers. They still made an important contribution to a more differentiated view of the significance of motives for social mobility: not only *between* but *within* social classes. Specific social position is deemed crucial to an individual's motives.

Goldthorpe and Lockwood called for research that goes 'beyond the mere surface description of "home-centredness", "money-mindedness", "status-striving" and so on', to find 'some understanding of how the behavioural patterns in question are related to, and take meaning from, the life-histories and life-situations of the individuals and groups concerned' (p. 142). They praised three independent studies on the perception of social class, conducted in 1957 in Germany, Switzerland, and England, that 'recognised that the problem of the "meaning" of respondents' statements on class and cognate questions could only be overcome by interpreting these statements in relation to respondents' overall perception, or image, of their society' (p. 145). These studies were 'dealing, in other words, with a *Gestalt*, not with a series of separate and unconnected responses' (p. 146, emphasis in original text). The authors believed in including the individual's social position and role in the division of labor into the analysis of motives crucial for social upward mobility. They also supported a change in research methods. Only special qualitative interview techniques can discover the individual motives embedded in social contexts for analysis. My research findings were collected and analyzed using this approach.

Turner (1964) showed that a wide variety of factors and circumstances are crucial for the creation of motives, or, as he called them, ambitions. To Goldthorpe and Lockwood's insight into intra-class differences in motives, he added social influences, such as gender. He followed Merton in assuming some general values, which he called society's values, and Goldthorpe and Lockwood in assuming that different classes prefer different values and thus have different motives. His merit consists in pointing out that classes differ in the *ease* with which they can attain society's values. Consequently, 'attainment of worldly success and community prestige may not cease to be a value but may be less salient in the value system of lower classes' (1962, p. 12).

He distinguished two paths toward upward mobility: a complicated one that extracts high costs in terms of the emotional suffering due to marginality, which he calls 'class consciousness', and an easier way, described as 'prestige identification'. In the former constellation, classes are highly segregated by demands of loyalty to mutually exclusive ingroups and outgroups. In the latter, loyalties follow other patterns than class membership. Another dimension that makes social ascent hard or easy is an anticipatory socialization that does or does not create aspirations. Turner saw the youth subculture as yet another dimension that influenced ambitions. He believes it was mainly independent of class, except for some traits that reflected a class affiliation: for example, the individualism more associated with the middle class. Gender plays a major role; men hold higher ambitions for social ascent than women, who are generally discouraged from upward mobility on their own.

In addition to their social contexts, Turner identified two broad types of ambitions: material and cultural. Material ambitions strive for such tangible goods as a house and a car, whereas cultural ambition emphasizes education. According to Turner, lower-class students prefer material rewards, and middle-class students educational rewards. However, he postulated this difference without relating it to actual differences in obtaining material resources between the classes. His study lacked data on *experienced* social upward mobility. The life histories in Chapter 4 fill this gap.

More recent social upward mobility research builds on these findings of differences in between-class motives to focus on motives within working-class members. Here, two main conclusions emerge, one emphasizing the importance of parents' aspirations and mainly mothers' support of their children, and the second, children and youths' desires and motivations to attain a college degree and/or to become a professional. In their study of 88 working-class children who made their way successfully through the educational system to become middle-class, Jackson and Marsden (1986) reported both very ambitious, supportive parent(s), mainly from wealthier working-class families in a mid-sized English town, and children's attitudes that positively influenced their ascent: 'The majority who lasted were those who, on the one hand, entwined academic ability with a positive orthodoxy and, on the other hand, had pressures behind them bearing on the school' (p. 171). Most of the educationally upwardly mobile children adopted the school's values. In some cases, they also consciously or unconsciously rejected their original social milieu, which some experienced as painful, and others did not.

Starting from the parents' aspirations, Gandara (1995) investigated social upward mobility during the 1960s and 1970s at highly regarded universities in the United States. Her study focused on 50 Mexican-Americans born between 1940 and the early 1950s who completed PhDs, MDs, and JDs. Their parents had low incomes, and fewer than a quarter held skilled jobs. Gandara found a great deal of support, especially from mothers, who created a 'culture of possibility' that imbued a strong will to ascend in their sons and daughters. However, the main reason why the participants in this sample obtained their doctorates was their own persistence. To this aspirational socialization, crucial opportunities were added: participation in a college preparatory course and the ability to access the information and resources needed to attend college.

Brendel (1998) conducted a qualitative study based on ten guided interviews (of total 25 interviews) with working-class daughters in Germany, one group who graduated from universities and the other who finished secondary school degrees and a vocational education.

Brendel started from hypotheses, abstracted themes, and created core assertions on each theme to which she ascribed the interviewee's portrait. She found that some, but not all, parents were education-friendly and supportive as well as daughters being motivated to move upward socially. Note that the daughters' motives were created mainly unconsciously by an identification with a positive view of the father's occupation and a negative view of the mother's.

Tepecik (2011) conducted a qualitative study on socially upwardly mobile children from ethnic minorities in Germany and reported that all of the families had a positive attitude toward education. Mothers and sisters were especially engaged in support, which in some cases led to a daughter's feeling that she had a duty to emancipate herself. In some cases, educational upward mobility was an opportunity for women to escape traditional gender roles for a while because they did not have to marry early, and they could move out of the home without risking a break with their families.

Kaya (2011) supported Tepecik's view. She also focused on ethnic minorities, interviewing three educationally upwardly mobile women whose parents are Turkish immigrants in Germany. Kaya added the hypothesis that, among the working-class Turkish community, ignorance and high estimation of the subjects of medicine and law led sons and daughters to select these atypical courses.

Siraj-Blatchford (2010) conducted case studies of underprivileged families from ethnic minorities in England whose children 'succeeded against the odds'. She speaks of the parents' 'concerted cultivation' of their children toward social upward mobility.

Finally, three studies move from the focus on parents' education to students' motivation. Rohleder (1992) closely aligned with findings relating women's educational upward mobility to parents' aspirations and support, as reported in Brendel and Tepecik's studies. Rohleder interviewed 13 female medical students from families that cannot be entirely categorized as working-class. Apart from good grades at school and other positive feedback that contributed to their confidence, their motives consisted mainly in the practical, hands-on elements of studying medicine, in contrast to humanities subjects, and their desire to be financially autonomous. All the women expressed their motivation to pursue medicine as a meaningful occupation in which they could help other people.

Lehmann (2008) picked up on the vocational dimension of university study that Rohleder mentioned by reporting on an investigation of first-generation students at the University of Ontario, Canada. They said that they chose to attend this university because they could get a rather vocational education and find a well-paying job. They did not relate their motivation to the more practically oriented subjects but to university study as a whole. Lehmann detected in their reasoning 'the uncritical acceptance of the knowledge-economy discourse' and noted 'how they discredit alternative post-secondary choices' (p. 141).

Alheit et al. (2008) studied nontraditional students at universities in Germany and offered four ideal patterns of their motives and practices. 'Patchworkers' are students who have tried several avenues in the past and who consider their decision to study another beginning. In contrast, 'ascenders' have wanted to study for a long time but were obstructed until now. 'Careerists' are somewhat similar to the extrinsically motivated students on whom Lehmann reports, characterized by their very strategic or instrumental attitude toward study. They are often well informed on ways to exploit their study and are often very successful. Finally, 'integrators' explicitly rely on their original capital to enrich their study experiences and often keep their distance from the university environment. The authors interviewed students in 1989 and 2005 and found that 'careerists' had increased, and 'ascenders' and 'integrators' decreased, within that period.

In sum, research findings on the significance of motives for social upward mobility show a curve from society-induced to individual motives. A major insight is the family-related creation of a specific motivation that results in a huge variety of working-class motivations for social upward mobility. In Chapter 4, I will clarify this stream of research by demonstrating how some interviewees' educational upward mobility is linked to their families' motivating socialization during periods of economic prosperity, and cultural and political openness to working-class participation in higher education.

1.2.2   Educational institutions and upward social mobility

Albeit closely linked to social structures, motives are mainly settled at the individual level, but upward social mobility is also influenced at the institutional level. Remarkably little research has reported empirical findings on educational institutions' contribution to upward social mobility, which might indicate that it is negligible among working-class people en masse. Like motives, the institutional level cannot be separated from the structural level. Turner's (1960) concept of contest and sponsored mobility might be categorized as a societal approach, because social norms play a crucial role. However, I classify it at the meso level of institutions, because he aimed to describe how educational institutions are shaped by social norms and affect social mobility.

Schools and universities both enable and impede social upward mobility. Turner demonstrated that the institution's influence on mobility depends on norms. 'The central assumption underlying this paper is that within a formally open class system that provides for mass education the organizing folk norm which defines the accepted mode of upward mobility is a crucial factor in shaping the school system' (Turner, 1960, p. 856). He found that norms work by imposing 'a strain toward consistency upon relevant aspects of the society. Thus the norm acts back upon the objective conditions to which it refers and has ramifying effects upon directly and indirectly features of the society' (Turner, 1960, p. 856). He called the predominant norm of upward mobility in the United States 'contest mobility', which 'is a system in which elite status is the prize in an open contest and is taken by the aspirants' own efforts' (p. 856). He called the predominant norm in Great Britain 'sponsored mobility', in which 'elite recruits are chosen by the established elite or their agents, and elite status is given on the basis of some criterion of supposed merit and cannot be taken by any amount of effort or strategy' (p. 856). Turner described the United States as generally a more open and democratic society, while British society is still organized according to monarchist principles. For him, norms secure control by maintaining loyalty. They 'must direct behavior into channels that support the total system'. Even people who 'transcend strata must support the general class differential' (p. 859). Otherwise, the total system would be altered, and social hierarchy could not be maintained. Country-specific mobility norms also secure disadvantaged class members' loyalty and conformity. 'In a system of contest mobility this is accomplished by a combination of futuristic orientation, the norm of ambition, and a general sense of fellowship with the elite' (p. 859). In a sponsored mobility society, like Great Britain's, control 'is maintained by training the "masses" to regard themselves as relatively incompetent to manage society, by restricting access to the skills and manners of the elite, and by cultivating belief in the superior competence of the elite' (p. 859).

According to Turner, the US educational system is less selective, and schools present an opportunity that depends mainly on the students' own initiative. In contrast, the British secondary school system of that time was highly selective. An examination at the age of 11 years decided whether pupils would attend grammar schools, which would prepare them for higher education, or secondary schools, mainly leading to vocational education. Turner stated that, in the United States, students who are less able receive a good deal of support to keep them in the contest, while, in the British school system, major funds are spent on grammar schools and little on secondary schools. University access in Britain is highly selective, but most students leave with a degree; it is more open in the United States, although many trials must be passed, and many people drop out.

Turner's view of the US system can be criticized as too positive; social mobility in a capitalist society is not based on effort alone but largely influenced by position and resources. What seems important in his approach, apart from extending the range of actors that shape social mobility, is its return to Merton's discussion of how social mobility is linked to the *maintenance* of social hierarchies. Turner found educational institutions to play a crucial role in enabling only *certain* upward mobility and, in large part, impeding it.

1.2.3 Societal factors for upward social mobility

Research on the societal factors that influence upward social mobility again seems rather limited. It can be organized by distinguishing studies pointing to societal circumstances that indirectly enable upward mobility from studies naming societal factors explicitly created to increase upward social mobility. In the first camp, Lipset and Zetterberg (1966 [1956]) summed up three structural developments supporting upward social mobility according to their literature review: differential fertility, an increase in white-collar positions, and a decrease in positions that could be inherited. Differential fertility refers to the observation that members of the upper social classes have fewer children than members of other classes, so opportunities that would have been available to the elite go vacant unless filled by others. The increase in white-collar positions is due to the decrease in manual jobs, and exclusively enables upward mobility for men, because the prestige of nonmanual jobs differs according to gender:

> It is true, of course, that many white-collar positions are lower in income and prestige than the higher levels of skilled manual work. Most of the less rewarded white-collar positions, however, are held by women. The men who hold them are often able to secure higher level supervisory posts. Consequently, we believe that using the division between manual and nonmanual occupations as indicators of low and high occupational status is justified as an approximate dichotomous break of urban male occupations. (p. 566)

Finally, the reduction in positions that could be inherited from father to son results from a general change in the occupational structure, a development in which 'the majority of nonmanual and high-status positions are no longer in the category of self-employment. A bureaucrat father unlike a business-man cannot give his job to his son' (p. 567).

Blau and Duncan (1967) partly agreed with this view, but applied a more differentiated approach. They noted that technological progress does not always or necessarily lead to an increased demand for higher skills, 'as exemplified by assembly-line production, which substitutes semiskilled operatives for skilled craftsmen' (p. 426). Weis (1990) applied a critical and much more detailed analysis of the new white-collar jobs emerging. She conducted an ethnographic study on the future plans of high school students and their parents' wishes for them in a former US steel industry town in 1985–6. It challenges Lipset and Zetterberg's view that the change from blue- to white-collar occupations should be regarded as *upward* social mobility. Weis investigated occupational changes for people who lived in a town previously dominated by a large, prosperous steel plant that went into decline during the 1970s and closed in 1982. She painted this picture of deindustrialization:

Factory closings are not restricted to the steel industry, and while more common to the northeastern United States, are not confined to this area. Gone are many jobs in heavy industry, automobiles, and manufacturing. The largest growth sector in the economy is now service, not production. Jobs in the service sector demand retraining, pay less, provide less security and fewer benefits, and often demand relocation. De-industrialization means a less secure, generally lower, standard of living for working-class Americans. (p. 6)

To Weis's material analysis of blue- and white-collar jobs, we should add a cultural analysis in which a country-specific evaluation of their respective tasks is related to social upward mobility. For example, in the United States as well as Britain, blue-collar work is much more devalued and disapproved of than in Austria or Germany, where certain areas of blue-collar work are prestigious and highly appreciated.

Here, Haller's (1989) critique of Lipset and Bendix's assertions about indirect societal factors contributing to upward social mobility is relevant. He asserted that all modes of mobility are specific to country, never general. He conducted a comparative study of class structures and mobility in Austria, West Germany, France, and the United States between 1930 and 1970 and found significant differences in their *modes* of mobility, closely linked to their class, social, and institutional structures (p. 355). Among the crucial institutional differences were their educational systems, forms of labor segmentation, and within-company distribution of, and hierarchies in, the workforce. According to Haller, these differences are linked to country-specific differences in social and political institutions aligned with the dominant value orientations and attitudes.

Goldthorpe et al. (1978) and Erikson and Goldthorpe (1992) raised another critique related to the actual extent of social mobility as a whole and not to single aspects. They found that the change in occupational structure related only to absolute, not to relative social mobility: while more people became white-collar workers, their social position in the societal hierarchy remained at the lower end. A comparative study showed that absolute mobility rates – the sheer number of people who change jobs – varied widely, while relative mobility rates seemed stable. The authors concluded that social mobility had not increased over time.

In this research strand on indirect societal factors, the assertion of change in the occupational structure and in the justification and legitimation of distributing positions leads to the conclusion that education becomes more important. Blau and Duncan found that the increased significance of education in industrialized societies was based on a hegemony of values and norms that push for rationality and efficiency. The authors called this fundamental trend *universalism*; it enters all spheres of life in industrial societies and replaces 'particularistic standards of diverse ingroups, intuitive judgements, and humanistic values not susceptible to empirical verification' (1967, p. 429). Unfortunately, they did not develop a more detailed analysis of this phenomenon and how exactly it relates to the change in the occupational structure. Universalism seems to resemble the universal motive Merton described as crucial for upward mobility, but, in contrast, Blau and Duncan did not consider that social norms of rationality and efficiency did not guide individual action, but were crucial for the creation of a whole societal epoch. Their main contribution to the analysis of social mobility was their methodological invention. They analyzed 20,700 men's responses to a questionnaire on their own and their fathers' education and occupations, which was a representative sample of the 20–64-year-old male citizens in the United States in 1962. On the basis of these data, they developed a new model of the stratification process, which shows path coefficients of social mobility that capture more variables than earlier bivariate tables. However, the authors clearly stated the limits of their model: 'The technique of path analysis is not a method for discovering causal laws but a procedure for giving a quantitative interpretation [describing associations or correlations] to the manifestations of a known or assumed causal system as it operates in a particular population' (p. 177).

On a much more concrete level, Weis (1990) analyzed how education became more important as reflected in human actions. She interviewed over 60 high school juniors, almost all teachers and school staff, and over 50 per cent of the students' parents, seeking their perceptions of current and future education and employment. Among the male students, Weis found that 40 per cent planned to go to a two- or four-year college. Manual-labor jobs were considered far less attractive. Among the female students, all but one girl 'made the obtaining of wage labor a *primary* rather than a secondary goal'

(p. 55, emphasis original). This response could be explained by the changing labor market, which absorbs women at a faster rate than men, although women still work mainly part-time, while men work full-time. As for the parents, 'they *desperately* want their children to attend college, and many state that there is nothing for their children if they do not do so. Parents understand clearly that the jobs in which they participated upon leaving high school are no longer available. They have lived through de-industrialization and stress to their children that education is the only way to obtain stable employment' (p. 151, emphasis original). Remarkably, parents' wishes do not differ between sons and daughters, but Weis made clear: 'Beyond stressing its [schooling] importance [...] there is little of a concrete nature that parents can offer their children' (p. 161). Overall, respondents perceived education as an almost purely extrinsic interest, leading to (good) jobs.

Some of the authors who propose the significance of education for upward mobility also question it. Blau and Duncan realized that in the United States education is used to secure privileges: 'Education assumes increasing significance for social status in general and for the transmission of social standing from fathers to sons in particular. Superior family origins increase a son's chances of attaining superior occupational status in the United States in large part because they help him to obtain a better education, whereas in less industrialized societies the influence of family origin on status does not seem to be primarily mediated by education' (p. 430). According to them, the universally established norm of rationality and efficiency makes education important to status.

Collins (1979) provided the most fundamental critique of the assertion that technological development and changes in the occupational structure require more and more highly educated people. He dismissed the technological relevance of education and offered the view that education is a cultural basis of group formation that shapes positions and careers.

We now turn to studies of societal circumstances that were designed to influence upward social mobility. Breen and Jonsson (2007) found that educational policies aiming to equalize the Swedish educational system increased social upward mobility. Their study was based on 24 annual surveys between 1976 and 1999, including 63,280 women and men born between 1912 and 1974. Their analysis showed that social class origin was less important for educational attainment in younger compared with older cohorts due to national educational policies, but social mobility only increased when the change in the educational system was considered in combination with a microsociological phenomenon: hiring practices that became more meritocratic over time. Breen and Jonsson believed that the change in hiring practices was based on overall educational expansion; employers had more well-prepared candidates to choose from. These findings point to the importance of societal-level policies that reduce social inequality in education as a prerequisite for social mobility.

A study by Stuart (2012) on first-generation higher education graduates employed in higher education in Britain linked their social upward mobility to domestic policy and economic changes. She differentiated cohorts according to incisive political and economic measures and conditions. The first, pre-1963, entered higher education before the Robbins Report, a government-initiated and crucial claim for the expansion of higher education in England. The 'golden period of higher education' ran from the mid-1960s to the end of 1979, when Thatcher became prime minister and a period of massification and reduced resources for universities took hold until the mid-1990s. In the last period she identified, from 1997 to 2007, fees were introduced. The study tightly connects the individual life histories of higher education students to the social contexts affected by higher education and welfare state policies and political decisions on higher education funding.

This overview of research on societal influences on upward mobility revealed a failure to consider cultural influences, such as the women's movements, and changing attitudes and lifestyles. My analysis of the life histories of educationally upwardly mobile people is aware of such cultural dimensions and adds them to enhance our understanding of the societal circumstances that influence social upward mobility.

1.3 Studies with other approaches to the subject of the educational upward mobility of working-class people

Many studies do not follow the micro, meso, and macro levels initiating or driving social upward mobility. Instead, they are mainly concerned with the experience of upward mobility among the working class and questions about how to increase its participation in higher education. I have divided these studies into five groups:

1. generally dealing with the experience of educational upward mobility;
2. focusing on the difficulties of social ascent;
3. focusing on certain working-class groups according to sexual orientation and profession;
4. addressing the question of sustainability of social upward mobility; and
5. addressing affirmative action and widening participation.

Of course, these groups overlap in various ways.

Please note that the following section focuses on educational upward mobility and not on social ascent in general. For the latter, see a study by Goldthorpe (1987) in which he analyzed short texts written by 247 men of different social backgrounds and classes, 101 of whom were upwardly mobile, on their perceptions and experiences. He found a lower degree of eagerness and effort among men of lower social backgrounds compared with the eagerness and effort *to maintain* a first-class position. Overall, these men evaluated social ascent positively and did not emphasize difficult or painful processes as in the studies introduced below.

1.3.1   Studies on experiences of educational upward mobility among the working class

Levine and Nidiffer (1996) described the complex lives and educational 'journeys' of 24 low-income students in the United States. Some gained admission to one of the most selective universities, and others studied at an open-admission two-year college. While students came from a wide variety of backgrounds and experiences, they had one thing in common: mentors who provided crucial support. These mentors were also diverse, ranging from parents to other family members, neighbors, teachers, coaches, guidance counselors, vocational counselors, human service officers, and therapists. Their educational backgrounds and methods of encouragement and support were diverse, too. However, the authors found four overlapping categories of support: mentors provided 'a sense of greater possibilities than they had imagined, and instilled in them a belief that those possibilities might be achievable' (p. 74); 'enhanced' their 'confidence' (p. 76); stressed the importance of education; and put 'them at the college gate. Whether figuratively or literally, these people put the student and the college together' (p. 77). Thus, Levine and Nidiffer recommended very concrete steps for early, local, individual mentoring, having consciously considered the weaknesses of this approach: 'it ignores root causes and accepts poverty as a continuing reality. Another limitation is that it is less ambitious, focusing on individuals rather than using a mass-market approach that emphasizes group or class' (p. 58).

Reay et al. (2010) examined the influence of four widely different academic places and spaces on working-class students' identities in the United Kingdom. They conceptualized the differences in terms of institutional habitus, exploring how it produces a range of experiences of fitting in or standing out. This mixed-methods study focused on learning and social experiences and analyzed data from 1,209 years 1 and 2 (undergraduate) student questionnaires, group and individual interviews, case analysis, and observations. Differences were pronounced among the 97 students they interviewed: some working-class students felt a sense of belonging to the middle-class higher education institution *and* to their homes, whereas others only partially absorbed a sense of themselves as students. In an earlier study, Reay (2001) described the opposing experiences of students from working-class backgrounds as 'finding or losing yourself' in higher education.

Hurst (2012) aimed to find out what college was like for US working-class students and focused on their experiences. In a second step, she widened her perspective by asking what college means to the working class as a whole, linking with the debate about working-class educational institutions, which has a long tradition but will not be pursued in this book.

1.3.2 Studies on the difficulties of social ascent for members of the working class

Studies focusing on the difficulties of social ascent relate closely to early studies on marginality, social anomaly, and deviance in the United States. For a German-speaking audience, Ortmann (1971) combined the concepts of Merton, Stonequist, and Hoggart with an analysis of empirical studies on students from lower social backgrounds in US colleges. She depicted social upward mobility as a painful process of suffering, usually leading to a bad ending. She saw the problems of social upward mobility for working-class members primarily as a mismatch between promised rewards and current sacrifices: 'Explanations of the consequences of social mobility so far point to a disconnection between the rewards promised by an ideology and the actual restrictions individuals must undergo. It follows that social ascent hardly enables the individual to reach emancipation in the sense of self-fulfilment' (p.141, my translation).

A large part of the research on the difficulties of social ascent, which could also be categorized as studies of special groups of social ascenders, addressed later, is written by female feminist social scientists. More women than men seem to study and write on this topic, for several reasons. First, female, more than male, socialization is directed at maintaining close family relationships, due to fewer concessions of individual freedom and expectations that she will put personal ambitions aside to assume care of ill or elderly parents and other relatives. Second, women have had to walk a long distance in these shoes; studies in Germany at the end of the 1960s identified the most educationally disadvantaged person as the rural, Catholic, working-class daughter (Pross, 1969).

Albrecht-Heide (1972) presented a study of social ascent at a so-called second-chance institution in Germany. She collected comprehensive data from the Braunschweig Kolleg on students, including their parents' backgrounds, their prior education, their experiences at the Kolleg, and later studies at universities. In her overall conclusions, she criticized the institution for deforming participants and thus maintaining rather than decreasing social inequality. Taking a psychological viewpoint, she called the change of role from young, autonomous, employed adults to dependent students regressive, but felt that the willingness to accept it eased the adaptation process. She emphasized that these students were not subject to deformation at the individual level, but on levels that individuals could not contest or amend.

Bublitz (1980) presented a comprehensive study of working-class daughters at universities in Germany. Like Albrecht-Heide, she evaluated educational upward mobility as an experience of deformation, composed of coercion to acquire knowledge from books written in inaccessible language and the focus on individual performance over solidarity, despite the increasing ideology of consumption. A third element was the way theory was taught, emphasizing abstract, formal, or idealistic content and contradicting working-class – especially daughters' – proclivity to acquire knowledge closely related to their experiences, their imagination, and their daily commonsense interactions with others. Finally, she found that universities characterized the sciences and other types of knowledge as developing and descending from above, as superordinate to human life, a perspective missing from working-class daughters' lives. Taken together, these features led to an experience of oppression, not liberation.

Theling (1986) interviewed 24 female students of education or social pedagogy at the University of Münster from 1983 to 1984 and found that many working-class daughters felt lonely. Not belonging to the middle class, yet no longer working-class, some described their isolation and disorientation. Several expressed the wish to work with working-class people once they finished their studies to increase their social contact with people to whom they felt close. Theling recommended that working-class students form groups to enable collective changes in their situation as a first step in overcoming the problem of isolation.

An anthology of texts by female feminists 'on the basis of their own experiences, of their confusion and ambivalence in locating themselves as "working-class" (Mahony & Zmroczek, 1997, p. 3) offers insights into various dimensions of the difficulties of social ascent. Note that their experiences are ambivalent, not restricted to difficulties or pain, but comprehend positive elements. For example, Clancy described her engagement in intellectual work: 'This chapter will explore how writers and writing, literature and reading, enabled me to leave my working-class roots and seek new identities in the alien, middle-class meccas of education, academia and the arts' (p. 44).

However, overall, the women's testimonies emphasize the difficulties. Coming from a German working-class background and having studied in England, Reinfelder stated: 'My relatives perceive me as "successful" (I don't) which produces admiration and resentment, both of which I find difficult to deal with' (p. 105). This discomfort holds true for women in academic positions, not just those holding a university degree, as Reay asserted: 'I suggest the female academic from a working-class background is unlikely ever to feel at home in academia' (p. 21), and the higher the position, the more intense the alienation. Skeggs was co-director of the largest Centre for Women's Studies in Britain: 'So, I now may occupy positions of power ... but I rarely feel comfortable. My experience is very similar to that documented by Valerie Walkerdine (1990), I feel a fraud, I feel that one day somebody will find out that I should not really be here' (p. 133). In an autobiographical narrative, Christopher (2009) reported her struggles as a carpenter's daughter switching classes in the United States.

Ingram (2011) reported on working-class boys' difficulties in dealing with two identities as they attended a grammar school in a working-class Belfast neighborhood. She observed three different year 11 classes, conducted one-to-one interviews, and held focus groups in which the boys were given modeling clay and asked to create two models. She found that they had problems in relating openly and comfortably with their families and neighborhoods, on the one hand, and their classmates, on the other. Her method may have contributed to her findings in that she asked them to produce two models, anticipating her finding of two separate identities.

Finally, I want to point to a study that specifies the *political* barrier working-class members have to face when they are educationally successful: 'By succeeding in college, working-class college students are not only embracing this type of work [middle-class work], but they are endorsing the hegemonic view that manual labour is *less worthy*' (Hurst, 2010, p. 5). Hurst interviewed 21 working-class students attending a large US public university mostly in two sessions between 2003 and 2005. She divided her sample into three groups: the '*Loyalists*, focusing primarily on the difficulties of fitting in at college and their discomfort with bourgeois values of competitive individualism, and *Renegades* focusing primarily on the shame and embarrassment they experienced when identified as working class or poor. ... A final group of students, *Double Agents*, stand somewhere awkwardly between these two poles' (p. 5, emphasis original). She stressed: 'The real threat our current educational system poses, however, is not that too few working-class students get to college, but that education favors inequality, competition, and hierarchy rather than solidarity, collective advancement, and equality, and that the few working-class students who get to college must forego these values in order to succeed' (p. 13). Hence, 'The competitive individualism required for social mobility through education is a doomed strategy for the working class to adopt' (p. 11).

Instead, Hurst considered two solutions: first, separating college from the labor market and, second, increasing the value of college for working-class students by offering skills useful for political change, such as collective organization and bargaining. In contrast, Goodwin (2002) observed a solution taking place on the individual level. She observed and interviewed 23 US working-class students, predominantly from urban public schools, now studying at an elite university with the help of the Higher Education Opportunity Program (HEOP). She posited their difficulties as a political problem, a problem of power: 'these students have been marginalized by oppressive power systems (Ivy University in this case) that function to preserve the dominant ideologies and status quo' (p. 210). She believed that their educational success relied on an individual strategy that can hardly be characterized as individual, since the interviewed students shared it: 'students construct systems of *strategic instrumentalism* that resist and oppose the institutionalized academic and social orders that frequently stigmatize and oppress them' (p. 210, emphasis original). Goodwin drew a picture of students who become 'resilient learners' by retaining their core identities *and* fulfilling formal requirements to proceed. Her later study (2006) supported the importance of resilience for educational success among disadvantaged students from three different types of migration backgrounds.

1.3.3 Studies on selected groups within the group of educationally upwardly mobile working-class people

Most studies on educationally upwardly mobile women emphasize difficulties, but an anthology edited by Schlüter and Borkowski (1992) focused on their strategies. In the Ruhr area in Germany, Schlüter interviewed nine female students from working-class families in male-dominated subjects: 'they were successful by distinguishing themselves from female stereotypes and by overriding social differences through relativisations. Relativisations cancel traditional ascriptions by emphasizing positive elements of experienced deficits (no money, but care; or no money, but becoming autonomous). This means, by exercising their own power of definition they gained freedom of action' (p. 119, my translation).

Prümmer (1992) studied working-class daughters at the largest distance-learning university in Germany (Hagen). She determined that they use their study to professionalize, to supplement their vocational education and the qualified occupation in which they are employed, and to increase their chances of social upward mobility. Goldman (2012 [1968]) edited a collection of 11 narratives by educationally upwardly mobile people, of whom all but two were occupied in the education sector, whether at universities or schools. Van Galen and Dempsey (2009) edited a collection of essays by educational scholars from working-class backgrounds, and Oldfried and Johnson (2008) edited an anthology on queer professors from working-class backgrounds. All three books rely mainly on personal narratives. In all three, educators play a crucial role in the narrators' development of processes to advance educationally. Melanie Nind observed in our personal communication that everyone has contact with teachers; the profession is universally familiar, so working-class people find it easier to relate to and aspire to than other, more distant professionals: for example, lawyers.

1.3.4 Studies on the sustainability of educational upward mobility

In 2007, a debate on the sustainability of social ascent through education took place in the well-known and prestigious German journal *Kölner Zeitschrift für Soziologie und Sozialpsychologie* (see Becker, 2007; Fuchs & Sixt, 2007a).The debate was predominantly methodological and will not be recounted here, but its findings over two and three generations demonstrate the importance of grandparents' education for their grandchildren's. Fuchs and Sixt (2007b) analyzed data from the Socio-Economic Panel Study (SOEP), an annual survey of 11,000 households and more than 20,000 persons by the German Institute for Economic Research (DIW), funded by the Federal Government and the Federal Land of Berlin. In this longitudinal study of private households, data on their composition, members' occupational biographies and employment, earnings, and health have been collected since 1984. Fuchs and Sixt found that children of educationally upwardly mobile parents did not obtain the same educational opportunities as children of parents who maintained the educational status of their own parents, the children's grandparents. In fact, children of educationally upward mobile parents obtained *fewer and lower* educational opportunities. A second result of the study demonstrated that children of parents who did not maintain the educational level of their parents *did not* sink to a lower educational level but were able to maintain the educational level of their grandparents, achieving a higher educational level than their parents.

1.3.5 Brief overview of studies on widening participation to increase the educational upward mobility of working-class members

Not many studies deal with the topic of widening participation, a policy introduced by the New Labour government to enhance participation in higher education in Britain at the end of the 1990s, in relation to the working class. Several focus on disabled people; many target the rather wide range of so-called nontraditional students; and some deal with aspects of learning and managing widening participation. A US study on black male undergraduates of whom 42 per cent had working-class backgrounds revealed the relevance of policy and specific university programs that enabled them to study at a range of colleges, some highly prestigious (Harper & Griffin, 2011).

The two studies presented here take up the question of widening participation among the working class. Bowl (2003) researched the Birmingham Reachout Project from 1997 to 2001. It focused on recruiting working-class *and* ethnic minority students to higher education. Part of New Labour's widening policy starting in the late 1990s, the core involved funding students but also included other dimensions of support, such as encouragement, which consisted in demystifying academia, building support networks, and breaking down hierarchies. Bowl summed up the overarching aim: 'The project attempted to build a bridge between its students and higher education, whilst also creating a safety net, which could support them if they faltered in their progress or if they were unable to find support within the university itself' (p. 164). Here, Levine and Nidiffer's (1996) finding on the importance of literally taking working-class people to the college becomes apparent.

In contrast, Burke (2002) had harsh criticism for the widening participation policy, finding that it failed working-class people and students at universities. The policy's discourse was oriented toward the 'standard' and 'normal' 18-year-old student, leaving out the majority of working-class students, who are older. Burke held that widening participation needed a 'methodology and pedagogy that give students a sense of ownership and control over research and learning processes' (p. 135) and did not treat them as passive objects. He criticized the current policy as counterproductive: 'Educational participation is constructed as an instrumental action within the neo-liberal project of individual progress and success through market opportunities. Yet access students often reject these instrumental notions of education' (p. 141). His findings opposed, for example, Lehmann's (2008), who found an extrinsic motivation for study among most of the first-generation students he investigated.

To conclude, widening participation generally seems to address and to support individual students, some of whom have working-class backgrounds, without seeking societal changes to increase participation of working-class people in higher education.

2
Theoretical Perspective

A theoretical outline is now necessary for two reasons. First, as working without a theory is impossible, the author must make as many of her assumptions explicit and transparent as possible. Second, a theoretical perspective enables us to go beyond sheer description of empirical data to explanation. We can offer an idea of a social phenomenon's structure and function.

Pierre Bourdieu and colleagues adhere to the first point. According to them, in sociology, all data and research objects involve theoretical presuppositions: 'An object of research, however minor or partial, can only be defined and constructed in terms of a *theoretical problematic* which makes it possible to conduct a systematic questioning of the aspects of reality that are brought into relationship by the question that is put to them' (Bourdieu et al., 1991, p. 35). In this study, for example, *educational upward mobility* is an expression of various theoretical problems entailing a concept of a hierarchically structured society characterized by higher and lower social positions, so that *mobility* is possible and *education* could lead to a change in social position. The literature review provided different theoretical assumptions about this topic.

Bourdieu et al. insist on a theoretically loaded description of data and, further, providing an explanatory theoretical framework, in contrast to the presumption that a description can be purely empirical. According to them, an epistemological approach that goes 'from the real to the general' (Bachelard, cited on p. 36) and represents a strong Western tradition of philosophy from Aristotle to Bacon is a trap: 'Reinterpreted in accordance with a logic that is none other than that of cultural borrowing, the scientific imperative of submission to the fact leads to pure and simple surrender to the given' (p. 37). The same might also be true for theoretical explanations, which must refer to previous thought, but I suppose the authors would reply that human minds are creative and can invent. In any case, we need theory to imagine a different world, which is a precondition for changing the world.

In relation to the second point, proposing that theory is not only inevitable but also fruitful, Bourdieu et al. point to practice, as they understand sociology as a strictly practice-oriented science. I am also mainly interested in practices, and therefore the next chapter outlines their guidelines on how to theorize, or how to practice theory. I will now explain why I consider Pierre Bourdieu's theoretical perspective most appropriate for my objective. I will present the parts of his theory that are relevant to this study, while refraining from giving a general introduction to his work, which has been done elsewhere (Grenfell, 2004; Harker et al., 1990; Robbins, 1991, 2000; Swartz, 1997).

2.1   Reasons for selecting Bourdieu's theoretical perspective

This study deals with the intersections of structure and agency. The life histories of people from working-class families who completed their studies at universities in Austria and Britain took place in, and were created by, social structures ranging from gender and class to national educational systems to specific regional cultures, such as rural heritage costumes, to labor divisions, to name just a few. They were also created by such individual actions as moving away from home, marrying, obtaining a vocational education, and receiving a grant. Individual actions take place in, and are created by, social structures, and social structures are created by individual and collective actions. For example, the decision to leave home for a young man is created and supported by his family and enabled by a residence for men in a society structured by a gender hierarchy that provides this option to men, whereas women are made to stay at home because they do not develop the desire to leave, they have no family support for such a decision, and residences for women are lacking. Thus, structure cannot be separated from agency, and, to analyze this topic, the theoretical perspective cannot divide them. Habitus, one of Bourdieu's central concepts, unites them, as I will explain in detail later.

A second feature of this study is my interest in class-specific contexts, which has two dimensions. First, I assume the existence of social classes, or social strata. An extensive debate continues over whether social classes still exist in such postindustrial societies as Austria and England, and whether the category of social class in social sciences should be replaced by the category of social strata (Crompton, 2008; Lareau & Conley, 2008; Wright, 2005). I am aware of the complex of problems involved in using the term *social class*, and I use it interchangeably with the term *social strata*, more common in German texts than in English.

Class-specific analysis of social contexts also requires appropriate theoretical tools. Bourdieu's social theory relies on the observation of social inequalities and an explanation of how they are created and maintained by power relations. His category of habitus links structure and agency, thus enabling the analysis of working or middle-class-specific behavior in different social contexts. In the chapters outlining the life histories of educationally upwardly mobile working-class members, I will point out social and class-specific contexts and actions.

A third reason why habitus serves as an appropriate category of analysis is this study's objective: to describe the processes of educational upward mobility among working-class members rather than to count their number and quantify outcomes. Habitus is a category that conceptualizes the processes by which attitudes, perceptions, and ways of thinking (logic) are transmitted and then guide actions. Therefore, it can serve as a tool to explain dynamic processes such as educational upward mobility.

A fourth reason for referring to Bourdieu's category of habitus is its openness to explaining social change. This reason might surprise some readers, as Bourdieu's theory has been accused, mainly in the Anglophone context, of being static, deterministic, and unable to deal with social change. However, I will quote from his work to prove that this critique expresses misunderstanding. Bourdieu himself (and with Wacquant) offered four explanations for explicit changes in habitus, although I do not think he elaborates on them or on processes of social change. He and Passeron (1971) cited as major reasons for upward mobility exceptional family milieu, exceptional abilities, and exceptional capacity to conform. However, they did not offer a systematic analysis of educational upward mobility, a gap that my study aims to fill.

2.2 Bourdieu's framework for the analysis of educational upward mobility among working-class people

This section will focus on the concepts of Bourdieu's social theory that are relevant to my analysis of working-class educational upward mobility. I will start with a very brief outline of his overall view on societies, which serves as a foundation for understanding his categories. I will then explain habitus as a theoretical category linking structure and agency, or macro and micro-sociology, and how it enables us to grasp class-specific behavior and agency. Moving in closer, I will explain why it is useful for describing and analyzing social processes. Finally, I will develop the possibility of using it to explain social change and sum up Bourdieu and colleagues' hints at the reasons for changes in people's habitus and, thus, social change.

2.2.1 Societies are stratified

Bourdieu's theory of society (*Gesellschaftstheorie*) adopts Marx's assumption that societies are organized in classes. Bourdieu's specific interest is in how the stratification of societies works. To my knowledge, he does not offer an explanation for it, which is why I understand it as a premise, not part of his analysis. He says that societal stratification is created and maintained through power relations. Here, educational systems are crucial in two ways. First, they are social areas of relative autonomy, with their own logic of talents, skills, performance, and meritocracy that, perhaps unintentionally, leads to a social selection that supports middle and upper-class students and discriminates against working-class students (Bourdieu & Passeron, 1977). Second, Bourdieu views education as an instance of social norms and values authorizing social hierarchies and providing a system of classification. As the main providers of education, schools function to convert collective heritage into an individual and collective unconscious (*Unbewusstes*), so students cannot understand how the content of their studies has been created and thus cannot question and change it (Bourdieu, 1983, pp. 138–9). Both dimensions of education maintain existing power relations and social hierarchies. Bourdieu uses the notions of *field* and *capital* to analyze social stratification. According to Rehbein and Saalmann (2009), his conception of field is very similar to Kurt Lewin's use, derived from the theory of magnetism: 'The core of the theory of field was the notion of a force that affects a body from a distance and thus defines the nature and limits of the field' (p. 99, my translation). The relationships of people in a field are characterized by power: 'Analytically speaking, a field would be defined as a net or configuration of objective relations between positions' (Bourdieu & Wacquant, 1992 p. 127, my translation). Here, we must acknowledge the assumption that people aim for high positions. Fred Hirsch (1977) created the concept of 'education as a positional good' based on the premise that people aim at obtaining higher positions than their fellows. Therefore, fields are areas of social struggle.

Bourdieu does not make clear how *field* and *social space* are related. However, in expanding on a Marxist account characterizing social stratification as a duality of up and down, he conceptualized social space as two dimensions: social position and lifestyle. The former mainly depends on material conditions of existence; the latter refers to tastes, habits, preferences, and attitudes. This duality enables him to define people's positions in fields or social spaces in two ways: the first is very similar to a Marxist perspective and analyzes material resources and position in the production process; but, in the second, people create their own positions, based on distinct lifestyles, which emphasizes agency (Bourdieu, 1998). The twofold dimension of position in fields relates directly to habitus. People obtaining a habitus enter and act within fields. Their habitus has an impact on their position in the field because fields are composed of specific rules; for example, schools work according to meritocratic rules. The rules are not neutral but have different effects on people with different habitus.

Finally, *capital* is another category relating to the stratification of societies and both field and habitus. It refers to the resources people obtain, described as economic, cultural, social, and symbolic capital, which influence their positions in fields both structurally and by distinctions that actors create directly. Bourdieu's theoretical categories are tools to analyze social stratification.

2.2.2   Habitus as a major theoretical concept for explaining the interrelationship of structure and agency

This section aims, first, to explain habitus in a general way, revealing why and how this category elucidates the educational upward mobility of working-class people. Then I will demonstrate how it helps to explain class-specific agency, social processes, and social change. Educational upward mobility takes place in specific social contexts. This study's focus is the national contexts of Austria and Great Britain between 1928 and 2012.

Bourdieu's theoretical perspective starts with a basic problem: 'that subjects indeed create their history themselves, but that the history at the same time opposes the subjects as an external power' (Krais, 1989, p. 47, my translation). Rehbein and Saalmann put this problem slightly differently: 'If practice is not a conscious adherence to rules or models, how can it be regular and consistent?' (p. 100, my translation). Bourdieu's objective is to grasp the interconnection of structure and agency.

He defines habitus as 'systems of durable, transposable dispositions, structured structures predisposed to function as structuring structures, that is, as principles which generate and organize practices and representations that can be objectively adapted to their outcomes without presupposing a conscious aiming at ends or an express mastery of the operations necessary in order to attain them' (1990, p. 53). As all human beings are socialized in specific contexts, they acquire certain views, norms, mentalities, and ways of thinking and acting. Here, the habitus of the family, neighborhood, village, and school works as a structure for the child embedded in them. Habitus defines how people perceive and deal with their environment over the course of their lives. In this sense, habitus is a dynamic structure of perceiving and dealing.

Habitus is a category that requires context-specific analysis of structures and agencies. Bourdieu defines class habitus as the 'subjective but non-individual system of internalized structures, common schemes of perception, conception and action, which are the precondition of all objectification and apperception' (p. 60). It is possible because 'The objective homogenizing of group or class *habitus* that results from homogeneity of conditions of existence is what enables practices to be objectively harmonized without any calculation or conscious reference to a norm and mutually adjusted in the absence of any direct interaction or *a fortiori*, explicit co-ordination' (pp. 58–9). A bit later he emphasizes the creation and maintenance of class habitus by class members' actions: 'The habitus is precisely this immanent law, *lex insita*, inscribed in bodies by identical histories, which is the precondition not only for the co-ordination of practices but also for practices of co-ordination' (p. 59).

Habitus is something everybody has, but it differs among social milieux. Thus, the habitus of people from the same class and similar social contexts is similar. Especially in *Distinction: A Social Critique of the Judgement of Taste*, Bourdieu offers a detailed outline of class-specific habitus, 'the "sense of reality", or realities, which is perhaps the best-concealed principle of their efficacy' (1990, p. 60). By 'sense of reality' he refers, for example, to the self-selection of working-class people not to enter higher education because they perceive universities as places where they do not belong.

For this study, the class-specificity of habitus has several meanings. First, few members of the working-class obtain higher educational degrees, especially compared with the middle and upper classes. Second, the educational pathways to higher degrees differ among working, middle, and upper-class members. Working-class paths are longer and stonier. Third, if members of the same class obtain a similar habitus, it attains the status of a presumption and is not in itself an object of my analysis. Consequently, I concentrate exclusively on working-class members who obtained higher education and do not compare their life histories with those of middle or upper-class members. The focus on working-class educational pathways to university degrees reveals the huge variety of life histories within one class, and again raises the question of theorizing society in social classes or clearly divided social groups. Bourdieu sees individual style in relation to the class habitus in these terms: 'Each individual system of dispositions is a structural variant of the others, expressing the singularity of its position within the class and its trajectory. "Personal" style...is never more than a deviation in relation to the style of a period or class' (1990, p. 60). My focus on working-class people captures the historically, politically, economically, and culturally decisive structures that supported their educational upward mobility better than a comparison with the middle and upper classes would.

Why is Bourdieu's framework especially suitable for understanding social processes? He offers his theoretical perspective, the practice-oriented way of knowledge, as an alternative to two other models: phenomenological and objectivist. He finds the phenomenological way of knowledge interaction-oriented and ethnomethodological; 'it considers the social world as a natural, self-explanatory given and does not question its self-referential definitions or the conditions of its own possibility. The objectivist way of knowledge (*Erkenntnisweise*) excludes analysis of the various conditions of the possibility of experience itself' (Bourdieu, 2009, p, 146). One essential part of his practice-oriented way of knowledge is analysis of the conditions of knowledge as part of knowledge. I understand this inclusion, not simply as a constructivist account of knowledge, but as a twofold process: grasping both what exists and how it is understood. Bourdieu's concept of habitus enables us to reveal, to analyze, and to explain social *processes* by emphasizing practice *and* dialectic. Practice and dialectic are both dynamic categories that intrinsically reflect processes, not static phenomena. Bourdieu defines his concept as a 'theory of the mode of creation of forms of practices' (2009, p. 164, my translation) and points to the '*dialectic between interiority and exteriority, this means, between interiorization of the exteriority and the exteriorization of the interiority*' (ibid., emphasis original, my translation). Note the dimension of practice, of creation, in interiorizing and exteriorizing. The analysis of educational upward mobility among working-class people in later chapters will discuss how the interviewees' life histories were shaped by actions, practices, interiorizing, and exteriorizing – all processes.

The capacity to apprehend social processes requires the dimension of change. The upward mobility of the interviewees' life histories expresses change, mainly in milieu; obviously change of milieu is embedded in societies where most working-class people do not obtain higher degrees. In this sense, social change must be distinguished from societal change, since change in the form of upward mobility relies on a socially unequal society. Still, the change is not personal; it relates to the structure of specific social contexts within which the educationally upwardly mobile people move and act. For this reason, the process can be identified and analyzed as social and not as a product of luck or personality traits.

One common critique of Bourdieu's concept of habitus is its alleged rigidity, its inability to capture change. However, the contrary is true: Bourdieu specifies habitus as 'a system of *long*-lasting (rather than permanent) schemes or schemata or structures of perception, conception and action' (2005, p. 43, emphasis original). Thus, the concept encompasses dynamic processes and can be used to analyze social change.

Bourdieu's view of human behavior can be taken as a premise that enables his readers to grasp habitus as a concept of change. He says that 'human behaviour is not monolithic. It is very open' (2005, p. 45). In the same place, he recognizes the 'danger of being seen as promoting the idea that human behaviour is monolithic and this is something that is sometimes said against the notion of habitus. But human behaviour is not monolithic. It is very open, very diverse, but within limits, and the idea of lifestyle is suited to express this loose systematicity which characterises human behaviour.' Others have taken Bourdieu's explanation of the *scope* of change as a negation of change. Elsewhere, he specifies the relationship between new and old: 'Because the habitus is an infinite capacity for generating products – thoughts, perceptions, expressions and actions – whose limits are set by the historically and socially situated conditions of its production, the conditioned and conditional freedom it provides is as remote from creation of unpredictable novelty as it is from simple mechanical reproduction of the original conditioning' (1990, p. 55). That is, habitus exists *between* robotic determinism and free play. Later, I will demonstrate that a more comprehensive analysis and understanding of social change must include the psychological dimensions of processing experiences.

In a text dealing mainly with art, Bourdieu (1983) describes how change – in this case, the emergence of an artist's basic creative patterns – can be explained by a systematic biography. He relates the change in style between two artists, on the macro level, to social structures, such as the urbanization that required large churches, and on the meso level, to structures such as the position of the artist in the clerical hierarchy. He argues for a *post festum* analysis of change, since it can only be conceived after it has been realized. This observation argues well for my study's methodology – the analysis of life histories – for capturing the change I am interested in, because it allows me to reconstruct the interviewees' experiences of educational upward mobility with hindsight.

Finally, I want to emphasize the dimension of change in the concept of habitus by relating Bourdieu's explicit answers to his critics. First, he argues against the claim that habitus is a closed circle: 'The habitus is not a fate, not a destiny. ... The model of the circle, the vicious cycle of structure producing habitus which reproduces structure *ad infinitum* is a product of commentators' (2005, p. 45). Rather, 'First, this closed circle is a *particular case*, namely, the case in which the objective conditions in which the habitus operates are similar to the objective conditions in which it is the product' (p. 46). As an example, he offers his analysis of gender hierarchies in *Masculine Domination* (2001). Without discussing whether this example is convincing, I note his second argument against the critique of habitus as a closed circle:

> even in traditional societies or in specific sectors of modern societies, habitus is never a mere principle of repetition – that is the difference between habitus and habit. As a dynamic system of dispositions that interact with one another, it has, as such, a generative capacity; it is a structured principle of invention, similar to a generative grammar able to produce an infinite number of new sentences according to determinate patterns and within determinate limits. The habitus is a generative grammar *but it is not an inborn generative grammar* as in Chomsky's tradition which is related to the Cartesian tradition. It is a principle of invention, a principle of improvisation. The habitus generates inventions and improvisations but within limits. (2005, p. 46, emphasis original)

I want to emphasize 'generative capacity' and 'structured principle of invention', which point to a capacity for change within bounds.

Bourdieu's third argument follows:

> in all the cases where dispositions encounter conditions (including fields) different from those in which they were constructed and assembled, there is a *dialectical confrontation* between habitus, as structured structure, and objective structures. In this confrontation, habitus operates as a structuring structure able to selectively

perceive and to transform the objective structure according to its own structure while, at the same time, being re-structured, transformed in its makeup by the pressure of the objective structure. This means, that in rapidly changing societies, habitus changes constantly, continuously, but within the limits inherent in its originary structure, that is within certain bounds of continuity. (p. 47)

Bourdieu emphasizes the scope, and thus the *limits*, of change, but does not deny change.

Here, I want to collect and summarize his assertions on the concrete catalysts of habitus change. I am leaving the purely theoretical possibility of change of habitus and turning to empirical examples. To my knowledge, Bourdieu mentions four catalysts: (1) a change in objective structures; (2) no actualization of habitus; (3) consciousness; and (4) pedagogic effort.

In *Pascalian Meditations* (2000, pp. 159–63), he explains how a change in objective structures can prevent actualization of habitus. He refers to situations of crisis or sudden change, as he observed among the Kabyle people in Algeria, some of whom experienced a feeling of displacement under the conditions of colonialism. Another example might be the German reunification, when former East Germans had to adopt dispositions other than the ones they had acquired and practiced before. In my view, the lack of actualization of habitus is linked to a change, not necessarily of objective structures, but of individual living conditions. The objective structures remain, but their *meaning* changes for the affected person. Hence, I do not subsume 'no actualization of habitus' under 'change of objective structures' as Bourdieu did.

Bourdieu sees habitus blocked when objective structures change. As noted, he found this phenomenon in his studies of Algerian society in the 1950s, which was characterized by a massive exodus from rural areas that differed tremendously from urban centers. The cities confronted the migrating Kabyles with a different life, a different economy, from the one they had grown up in and were used to. The actions and behavior appropriate to their more family and exchange-oriented economy did not work in the cities and led to failures. They were exposed to different objective structures and had to acquire a different lifestyle to survive. Obviously, the large gap between rural and urban life was part of a more general process of modernization and the final stage of colonization in Algeria, conceived as changes in objective structures. However, in another sense, the objective structures continued, and the lack of actualization of habitus among those who moved into them can be attributed to forces at a more individual level, but not at a personal or private level. When living conditions alter a person's social status, objective structures, although unchanged, have a different meaning and impact.

In Section 4.3, I will illustrate this point in the life of a woman whose divorce led her to higher education. Her social status had been tied to her husband's. With the divorce and under objective structures that favored married over single people, gender-specific division of labor to gender equality, and the cultural value of marriage as part of a good life, she had to realign, to work out a new life perspective, an alternative path to an income and social respectability. She experienced a lack of actualization of habitus, perceiving objective structures *differently*, which ultimately led her to educational upward mobility. Objective structures have different meanings under different circumstances, and a change in circumstances can foster a different habitus.

In *An Invitation to Reflexive Sociology*, Bourdieu and Wacquant (1992, p. 137) propose that people can change their habitus by becoming conscious enough to control their dispositions. Once people become aware of the mechanisms that create the categories of perception and evaluation that condition their attitudes and behavior, they can gain distance from and escape them. 'It is difficult to control the first inclination of habitus, but reflexive analysis, which teaches that we are the ones who endow the situation with part of the potency it has over us, allows us to alter our perception of the situation and thereby our reaction to it' (p. 136). In Section 4.4, I will report a life history in which a process of becoming conscious permitted educational upward mobility.

Finally, in his paper 'Habitus', published in the anthology *Habitus: A Sense of Place* (2005), Bourdieu mentions a fourth catalyst for change: pedagogical effort (p. 45).

There is another difference which follows from the fact that the habitus is not something natural, inborn: being a product of history, that is of social experience and education, it may be *changed by history*, that is by new experiences, education or training (which implies that aspects of what remains unconscious in habitus be made at least partially conscious and explicit). Dispositions are long-lasting: they tend to perpetuate, to reproduce themselves, but they are not eternal. They may be changed by historical action oriented by intention and consciousness and using pedagogic devices. (One has an example in the correction of an accent of pronunciation.) A linguistic habitus, for example, is a product of primary education and cannot be corrected completely despite all one's efforts. It is the same with any kind of ethical habit. Any dimension of habitus is very difficult to change but it may be changed through this process of awareness and of *pedagogic effort*. (p. 45, my emphasis)

Bourdieu does not specify whether he is referring to 'pedagogical effort' in the sense of symbolic violence – that is, an alienated situation in which people are exposed to indoctrination and training – or in a positive sense of supporting people to become aware of their situation and to escape alienation. Since he mentions the 'process of awareness and of pedagogic effort' together, the positive interpretation may be more plausible. Among my interviewees' paths toward educational upward mobility, I also found pedagogic effort, which will be described in Section 4.5.

Thus, I found all four catalysts of habitus change in the interviewees' life histories, and when I am discussing their educational upward mobility I will return to Bourdieu's suggestions. Overall, equipped with his theoretical perspective, I will apply his categories to my analysis of educational upward mobility.

3
Study Methodology

This study is based on 18 interviews; almost all participants were from working-class families and all obtained university degrees, 12 in Austria and six in England. The term *working class* is used here to describe people whose parents are included in categories 7–10 of the European Socio-economic Classification (ESeC; see Institute for Social and Economic Research, 2013), ranging from lower-grade white collar to semi-skilled and unskilled workers and long-time unemployed. Since the ESeC focuses on occupation, and education informs an individual's socioeconomic status, educational lev`els are included in our definition of *working class*. Only educational achievers whose parents' educational qualifications stop at the International Standard Classification of Education (ISCED) level 3 – in England, the Higher Education Access Courses level and, in Austria, secondary-level vocational education – are included in this study (UNESCO, 2013). In short, *working class* refers here to people in lower occupational positions with educational qualifications below tertiary level and to their children. I am aware of the lengthy discussion of the term and the difficulties of clearly categorizing it as a social group. Instead, I adopt this rather technical definition because it is used in statistics to count the number of working-class people in higher education. From the sample introduced in Section 3.4, it clearly covers a large range of socioeconomic backgrounds *within* the working class.

To analyze the interviews, I used parts of Rosenthal's method for analyzing biographical narrative interviews (1993, 2004, 2008). In Britain, Chamberlayne and Wengraf participated in workshops with her and made her method known (Chamberlayne et al., 2000, 2002, 2004; Chamberlayne & King 1996, 2000; Wengraf, 1999, 2001). While relating to their publications for this English treatment might have been easier, I prefer Rosenthal as the source.

3.1 Reasons for using Rosenthal's method to study educational upward mobility

Rosenthal (2008) sees three areas of cognitive interest for inter-pretative social research: the unknown; interdependencies (*Wirkungszusammenhänge*); and latent meaning. Educational upward mobility has mainly been investigated by quantitative methods, or, where qualitative methods were applied, the focus was mostly limited to a certain period in the subject's life. Thus, the biograph-ical approach is still widely unknown in this area, and quantitative methods would require prior knowledge to develop the right tools for investigation. The extensive literature on the difficulties, barriers, and discrimination working-class members face in education revealed reasons and mechanisms for excluding them, but we still know very little about what enabled them to graduate from universities and what educational pathways they took.

The biographical approach is also especially apt for exposing inter-dependencies between social structures and agency in the social contexts in which educational upward mobility took place. Finally, because educationally upwardly mobile people are not necessarily conscious of the circumstances that enabled their trajectory, recon-structing their life histories enables me to discover and reveal the latent meaning of conditions that supported their mobility.

I want to mention that Bohnsack (2003), in conjunction with Mannheim, developed a method very similar to Rosenthal's, known as the 'documentary method'. It aims mainly to reveal the organi-zation of unconscious orientations and knowledge that have been crucial for the interviewees' lives. By setting up focus groups, the researcher can analyze the participants' frames of reference, which indicate wider social frames of orientation. In my view, we can reach the same result with Rosenthal's method, as it includes analysis of social contexts: here, frames of knowledge. Further, in contrast to Rosenthal, Bohnsack (2003, 2007) does not leave the empirical framework of the interviewees' knowledge to seek insights beyond it, which Bourdieu (2009) claims is necessary for *scientific* social *theory*. Therefore, Rosenthal's method provides a wider scope, and, in addition, I prefer individual interviews to focus groups – they give the subjects more uninterrupted time to narrate their life histories and offer deeper insights.

3.2   Connecting the Bourdieu perspective on research practice to the Rosenthal method

Key to Rosenthal's methodology is the 'reconstruction' of life histories. The complicated procedure of analysis, outlined in the next section, can go beyond a mere description of the interview's textual content. The researcher's perspective and findings will differ from the interviewee's perspective because they include it. The researcher deals with both the narration, which relates life events, and why it was presented as it was, of which the interviewee is unlikely to be aware. The analysis also reflects on the situation of the interview, distinguishing between the content and the context of narration.

This process can be seen as a first step toward what Bourdieu describes as the pathway to recognition (*Erkenntnisweise*): 'a *disruption* of all preconstructed representations and previously created classifications and official definitions' (2009, p. 149, my translation, emphasis original). He continues: 'Obviously, one could aim to create an account of an account, but only under the condition that one does not mistake a prescientific representation of the social world for a contribution to the sciences or as science of this social world' (p. 149, my translation).

According to Rosenthal, reconstructing life histories reveals the 'rule' of materialization of the life history, genetic material, and structures that created them: 'Building a type in this gestalt-theory/structuralist understanding means analyzing the gestalt of the social occurrence under study ... and reconstructing the fundamental rules of its constitution and not, as in descriptive type-building, tying together a few remarkable criteria' (2008, p. 76, my translation). Bourdieu and Passeron (1977) state that reconstruction is a way to make sense of class-specific educational processes: 'Experiences which analysis is able to distinguish and specify only in terms of the intersection of logically permutable criteria cannot be integrated into the unity of a systematic biography unless they are reconstructed on the basis of the original class situation, the point from which all possible views unfold' (p. 89). Elsewhere, Bourdieu and colleagues point to the difference between similarity and analogy: 'Playing on the confusion between simple *resemblance* and *analogy* – a relation between relations that has to be won against appearances and constructed by means of abstraction and conscious comparison – *mimetic models*, which grasp only the external similarities, are opposed to *analogical models* aimed at apprehending the hidden principle of the realities they interpret' (1991, p. 53, emphasis original). Rosenthal also aims to reveal interdependencies and latent meanings. Both aim at revealing structures that recreate the object under study. Therefore, although Bourdieu et al. dismiss the sociological stream of phenomenological knowledge with which Rosenthal would be identified and oppose phenomenological knowledge to praxeological knowledge, I think their similar objectives outweigh their differences.

By combining the perspectives of Bourdieu and Rosenthal, we can offer explanations for lifestyle changes. While Bourdieu provides the theoretical categories relevant to describing lifestyles, Rosenthal provides methodological instruments to grasp their processes in life histories. Taken together, changes in individual lives embedded in social contexts and structures can be described *and* explained, and the shortcomings of lifestyle typologies that Otte (2004) criticizes can be overcome.

3.3 Rosenthal's method of analysis of life histories

The most important assumption that Rosenthal shares with other social scientists engaged in interpretative research is that the world has already been interpreted. This view aligns with Bourdieu's assertion that all research topics are theoretical and opposes the view that the social world is an object unaware of its meaning.

The view of the social world as an interpreted reality signifies that it is constituted by interactions that depend on the participants' interpretations, which depend on a socialization with interaction rules and structures that are interpreted according to each biographical situation. Social reality is produced when participants define situations as real. In terms of data collection, the reality of the situation – for example, the interview – is created by interviewers and interviewees. This perspective must be taken into account in the interview analysis.

3.3.1   Five principles for analyzing interviews

Rosenthal defines five principles for analyzing interviews. The first is openness (2008, pp. 48ff). It aligns with the explorative character of research into what is almost unknown and is expressed during data collection as well as hypothesis creation. Generally, an initial open question to the interviewee functions as an invitation to narrate. The interviewer has no further prepared and fixed questions, but additional questions arise during the course of the interview while listening. The interviewer does not analyze the material with elaborated categories or hypotheses, but creates hypotheses during the analysis. Here, the reader may think that this method contradicts Bourdieu's claim that a nontheoretical analysis is impossible, but Rosenthal's method invites the researcher to reflect on theoretical understandings of the analysis later, when creating hypotheses, and then to check them with the text. However, Rosenthal explicitly names her method *abduction*, while Bourdieu favors *deduction*.

Hypothesis creation during analysis is tied closely to Rosenthal's second principle, the importance of the whole context for the interpretation of single parts: 'Each text is being interpreted anew, the meaning of single parts are being reconstructed within the whole context of the text' (2008, p. 57, my translation). Thus, the interview text is perceived as a 'consistent entity' that 'is created by the fundamental system of rules' (p. 57), and the objective of reconstruction is to reveal the 'rule of structuring' that created each instance of educational upward mobility.

The third principle is abduction (p. 58). Its key feature is to generate and to check hypotheses case by case and not to deduce from theories or hypotheses to testable consequences (deduction) or to search for indices or proofs and evidence for an already existing hypothesis (induction). Again, note that Bourdieu's argument for the inevitability of a theoretically driven, thus deductive, approach differs from Rosenthal's understanding of deduction as a conscious decision to support a particular theoretical perspective. Since Bourdieu and Rosenthal understand theory-related research differently, they do not contradict each other. In my own study, I diverge from Rosenthal at this point because I consciously selected Bourdieu's theoretical perspective as the most useful framework. However, I am not testing his theory but, rather, using it abstractly, as a perspective on society. In Rosenthal's abductive process, the explanatory hypothesis develops with the analysis of the interview.

The fourth principle is sequentiality (pp. 71ff), which implies that the interview text has a meaningful shape and cannot be reorganized to analyze – or invent – 'themes'. The analysis considers the placement of single passages within the whole texture to be important. Finally, Rosenthal's fifth principle is theoretical generalization (pp. 74ff), or building types from singular cases. It does not refer to any numerical assertions, such as frequency of occurrence, but to finding structures by dissociating case-specific details. A type of a case is designated by the rules that created it and should be understood as a model. Diverging from Rosenthal, I demonstrate how contexts and circumstances enabled educational upward mobility without creating types.

3.3.2 Six steps for analyzing an interview

According to Rosenthal (1993, 2004, 2008), the analysis of biographical narrative interviews aims to reconstruct the case. Interviewees narrate past incidents, and interviewers must remember that they are not experiencing what happened; their subjects can only relate the way they perceive the past at the moment of the interview, which influences the way they narrate it. To come closer to what actually happened and why it is narrated in this way, the level of experience must be distinguished from the level of narration.

Each interview is analyzed in six steps. The researcher starts by defining the chronological order of the biographical data. A kind of CV forms, and, second, to each biographical datapoint, such as date and location of birth or entrance to school, the researcher adds general background, such as information on the village where the interviewee was born, and postulates how this place and time would influence the interviewee's life as a whole.

Third, the interview is divided into sequences. A sequence is a coherent section on one topic. For each, the researcher notes the content and how it was presented: for example, factually or emotionally. The resulting table enables the researcher to gain a quick purchase on the large amount of material and an overview of which content (experience) is narrated in what way.

Fourth, the researcher focuses on the level of narration, generating hypotheses about why each sequence is presented in *this* way and not another, which reveals possible themes and thematic fields that point mainly to the social contexts in which the experiences took place. The researcher must also ask why the content is introduced in this sequence, which areas of life are mentioned and which are left out, why the content is presented in detail or tersely, and other questions about style and affect.

Fifth, the researcher returns to the level of experience and falsifies, proves, or creates a new interpretation of the biographical data by looking up all the sequences in the interview text that are related to the biographical data analyzed in the second step. At this stage, the reconstruction of the case takes place. By looking up all sequences dealing with a topic, the researcher can use the interview material to prove the validity of the initial hypotheses. If they were wrong, now the life can be reconstructed by analyzing various sequences together. The whole analysis, but especially the detailed parts, should be discussed with other researchers to correct or confirm and thereby strengthen it.

In the sixth step, the narrated life history is contrasted with the experienced one. This step enables the researcher to reveal the rules of difference between the narration and the experience, and the rules that created this presentation, and to explain the genetic process of this case. On this basis, a type can be formulated.

Clearly, such an analysis of one interview is a highly complex and time-consuming procedure, requiring several weeks. It achieves very vivid descriptions of social milieux and individual actions in social contexts. It enables the researcher to trace educational upward mobility through subjective meanings, worldviews, and how they were created and articulated. Finally, it enables theory building. Bourdieu et al. describe a theoretical model more as an instruction to theorize: 'Thus the *theoretical model* is characterized by its capacity for breaking with appearances and its capacity for generalization, these two qualities being inseparable. It is a formal outline of the relations among relations that define constructed objects, which can be transposed to phenomenally very different orders of reality' (1991, pp. 54–5). Rosenthal's six-step method repeats this layering and transposition of relations. I diverge from it, mainly replacing the sixth step, emphasizing people, with a strong emphasis on describing the social contexts in which educational upward mobility took place. Nevertheless, the method enables a profound and comprehensive analysis of interview texts by inviting the researcher to collect additional information and to test the validity of hypotheses systematically and frequently.

3.4 Study sample

Data collection took three years, from 2009 to 2012. I started in Austria, where I was living, and continued in England, where I later moved and conducted more interviews. Although the selection of countries was personal and practically determined, the comparison has several scientific merits. First, their educational systems, labor markets, and welfare state and educational policies differ, enhancing the range of social contexts enabling the educational upward mobility of working-class people. These differences are sketched in Table 3.1.

Interviewees were recruited using the snowball system and, in Austria, an announcement was placed in a journal for alumni of an evening school, which is a second-chance educational institution for adults to study for the highest school-leaving degree, the *Matura*, which provides full access to all subjects of study in tertiary education and corresponds to ISCED level 3; to be more specific, category 34, indicating upper secondary general education, and subcategory 344, indicating a sufficient level for direct access to tertiary education. Later, I will use such specific numbers to indicate precisely the educational categories of interviewees' parents. Several alumni contacted me after having read the announcement and agreed to narrate their life histories. In this sample, I included people whose parents could both be categorized as working class following the European socioeconomic classification. I also included people who had spent their whole formal education in either Austria or England (one exception spent a semester abroad) and had no background of migration. Table 3.2 provides an overview of the sample following year of birth, an important category for upward social mobility, in chronological order.

Table 3.1 Comparison of Austrian and English educational systems, labor markets, and welfare regimes

Austria	England
Highly stratified school and educational system	Formal comprehensive school system; reputation of particular educational institutions is crucial
Coordinated market economy*	Liberal market economy
Conservative welfare state†	Liberal welfare state

Notes: *Coordinated and liberal market economy are 'Varieties of Capitalism' classification categories created by Hall and Soskice (2001).

†Conservative and liberal welfare states are categories created by Esping-Andersen (1990).

Table 3.2 The sample

Birth year	Pseudonym Gender	Country	Parents' education, occupation, and ISCED and ESeC categories where appropriate	Year of graduation from university	Most crucial enabling circumstance(s) and section(s) where mainly described
1928	Georg Amlang Male	Austria	Mother: no information on education; day laborer (ESeC 9) Father: skilled carpenter; ill and unemployed (ISCED 453, ESeC 10)	About 1965 State examination in law	4.2.1 National Socialism as way to escape poverty 4.2.2 Modernization of Catholic Church as means to upward social mobility
1931	Gerhard Moser Male	Austria	Mother: compulsory school; housewife (ESeC 10) Father: skilled miller, miner (ESeC 9)	1957 Diploma, agricultural engineer	4.1.4 Poor material conditions and educational affinity
1939	Erwin Radler Male	Austria	Mother: compulsory school; household help, industrial worker (ESeC 9) Father: skilled scythe smith; partly captive (ISCED 453, ESeC 8 and temporarily 10)	1967 Diploma, engineer in technical physics	4.1.4 Poor material conditions and educational affinity
1941	Hans Pellar Male	Austria	Mother: probably compulsory school, farmer (ESeC 5)* Father: probably compulsory school, farmer (ESeC 5)	1971 Doctorate in veterinary science	4.2.3 Modernization of agriculture and immense loss of jobs 4.6.1 Contribution of being male to educational upward mobility 4.7.2 Evening school

1953	Andrew Lewis Male	England	Mother: compulsory school; maid, cleaner, housewife (ESeC 9, 10)	1976 BA Hons. in History	4.5 Pedagogical effort leading to educational upward mobility
			Father: compulsory school; factory worker (ESeC 9)	1990 Diploma in Careers' Guidance (a 1-year postgraduate, full-time diploma)	
1954	Renate Steiner Female	Austria	Mother: compulsory school; housewife (ESeC 10)	2007 Master's in law	4.7.2 B-*Matura* and evening school
			Father: compulsory school; bricklayer (ESeC 8)		
			Grandmother: went to a convent school, not clear for how long; house owner (ESeC 10)		
1954	Christine Gruber Female	Austria	Mother: probably compulsory school; housewife (ESeC 10)	1977 Diploma in *Wirtschaftspädagogik* (mix of economics, business studies, and pedagogy)	4.2.4 Working-class-friendly educational policy
			Father: skilled accounting clerk (ISECD: 453, ESeC 7)		

Continued

Table 3.2 Continued

Birth year	Pseudonym / Gender	Country	Parents' education, occupation, and ISCED and ESeC categories where appropriate	Year of graduation from university	Most crucial enabling circumstance(s) and section(s) where mainly described
1957	Alice Clayton Female	England	Mother: compulsory school; pastry cook, cleaner, hospital porter (ESeC 9) Father: compulsory school; manual laborer at building sites (9)	2007 BSc in Outdoor Recreation 2010 PGCE (Postgraduate Certificate in Education)	4.3 Lack of actualization of habitus as catalyst for educational upward mobility
1960	Oliver Berry Male	England	Mother: education and occupation unknown (ESeC most likely 9 or 10) Father: education unknown; lorry driver, works in a pub (ESeC 9) Grandparents were guardians; landowners (ESeC 5)	1992 BA Hons in Arts 2003 MSc in health policy	4.8.1.2 Great upheavals in childhood and finding orientation in higher education
1960	Scott Johnson Male	England	Mother: compulsory school; cleaner (ESeC 9) Father: compulsory school; bank messenger (ESeC 9)	2005 BA General from Open University 2009 BSc Hons in Maths	4.1.2 Materially secure living conditions enabling long perspective for upward social mobility 4.1.3 Lifestyle in childhood: a loving atmosphere enabling educational development

1960	Peter Mutz Male	Austria	Mother: compulsory school; maidservant, agricultural laborer (ESeC 9)	1990 Master's in Economics	4.8.1.1 Abandonment overcome by logical capability acquired in higher education
1964	Eric Finch Male	England	Father: skilled merchant in retail (ESeC 7) Mother: compulsory school; secretary, manual worker in shoe factory, perfume factory (ESeC 9)	1985 BA Hons in Peace Studies	4.1.1 Parents' backgrounds as motors for children's educational upward mobility
			Father: compulsory school; millworker, kitchen worker, transport worker (ESeC 9)	1993 MSc (Econ) in Applied Social Science and a Diploma in Social Work (DipS.W.)	4.1.2 Materially secure living conditions enabling long perspective 4.6.1 Contribution of being male to educational upward mobility
1966	Claudia Stangl Female	Austria	Mother: compulsory school; low-level secretarial course, housewife (ESeC 10)	1989 Master's in sociology	4.1.1 Parents' backgrounds as motors for children's educational upward mobility
			Father: skilled carpenter, works in carpentry as civil servant in jail (ESeC 8)		4.1.2 Materially secure living conditions enabling long perspective 4.1.3 Lifestyle in childhood: a loving atmosphere enabling educational development

Continued

Table 3.2 Continued

Birth year	Pseudonym Gender	Country	Parents' education, occupation, and ISCED and ESeC categories where appropriate	Year of graduation from university	Most crucial enabling circumstance(s) and section(s) where mainly described
1966	Friedrich Schrieben Male	Austria	Mother: skilled shop assistant, waitress (ESeC 9) Father: skilled metal worker, train driver (ESeC 8)	1999 Master's in social economy	4.1.2 Materially secure living conditions enabling long perspective 4.7.3 Upper secondary vocational schools providing direct and comprehensive access to higher education
1966	Alexander Mair Male	Austria	Parents' education and exact occupation unknown but ESeC 7 at highest	1992 Master's in engineering in mechanic technology in metallurgy	4.1.2 Materially secure living conditions enabling long perspective 4.7.3 Upper secondary vocational schools providing direct and comprehensive access to higher education
1968	Beth Rogers Female	England	Mother: compulsory school; shop assistant (part-time) (ESeC 9) Father: education unknown; plumber (ESeC 8)	1990 BA (Hons) in English Literature and Religion	4.4 Becoming conscious as a motor to change habitus

1972	Karin Eichner Female	Austria	Mother: compulsory schools; factory worker, cleaner, packer in retail (ESeC 9)	2000 Master's in sociology	4.8.1.3 Overcoming neglect by finding herself in higher education
			Father: education unknown; taxi driver (ESeC 9)		
1978	Stephanie Wollner	Austria	Mother: compulsory school; cleaner (ESeC 9)	2005 Master's in social economy	4.1.1 Parents' backgrounds as motors for children's educational upward mobility
	Female		Father: skilled carpenter; civil servant at post office (ESeC 7)		4.1.2 Materially secure living conditions enabling long perspective for upward mobility

Note: *Pellar might be considered an exception because his parents are classified above working class. I included him because of their low income and educational levels, considered in German-speaking countries as key for children's educational paths, more so than their occupations.

4

Social Contexts Enabling Educational Upward Mobility

Educational upward mobility is a phenomenon of social change. It is embedded in, and initiated by, changing social structures, such as modernization. Furthermore, it is itself a social change because individuals leave their original milieux and enter new ones. The way they raise and educate their children differs from the way they, as socially mobile people, were raised and educated; their work and lifestyles differ from those of their parents, siblings, neighbors, friends, and classmates. This chapter highlights social change by pinpointing what enabled it: when and where something new started in the life histories of my interviewees.

My aim is to demonstrate how social circumstances enabled educational upward mobility. Therefore, departing from Rosenthal, I do not present types of educational climbers but the social conditions that were crucial for their trajectory. By explaining their life histories, I will show how specific social conditions affected them and enabled *them* to move upward. I will demonstrate the highly complex and dynamic process in which macro, meso, and microsociological levels interrelated to enable educational upward mobility. I want to refute the contention that personality traits are the basis of educational upward mobility and, instead, point to crucial social contexts. Deep emotional and psychological processes contribute, and I will address them in detail at the end of the chapter. However, they arise in a social context, and my social analysis of them aims to expose the social dimensions of educational upward mobility.

One result of my study shows that no single social factor ever dictates educational upward mobility. Instead, one enabling social circumstance links to another in a complex scaffold. Presenting these findings is difficult, as matching a clear set of social circumstances with a clear set of individual outcomes is impossible. I cannot develop a manual or tips to achieve educational upward mobility. For each individual, two or more social circumstances were crucial. My description, therefore, will focus on the social circumstance that I consider most important for that individual, and I will explain the life as necessary to understand its impact on this individual's social upward mobility. This approach necessitates describing the same life history more than once, but the focus on the social circumstance enabling the upward mobility should counter repetition.

I found eight areas of social circumstance crucial for educational upward mobility:

1. socialization;
2. change in objective structures;
3. lack of actualization of habitus;
4. consciousness;
5. pedagogical effort;
6. gender;
7. educational institutions' support for inclusion; and
8. truth-seeking.

Numbers 2–5 are Bourdieu's suggestions for the conditions that change habitus, and number 8 emphasizes a mindset. I include it because it was clearly important among my sample and points to a dimension of the concept of habitus – the human mental agency embedded in social structures – that Bourdieu did not address, and thus it enhances his concept of habitus.

I will explain all eight areas in order, starting with socialization, to show how a certain kind of socialization in working-class families leads to educational upward mobility. Here, my findings echo a study by Jackson and Marsden (1986) that found many among their sample of educationally successful children lived in homes where parents were very supportive.

4.1   Socialization

Among the whole sample of 18 interviewees, a loving, supportive, and education-friendly socialization embedded in secure living conditions was decisive for eight people. I will first describe the socialization of a core of six, which was characterized by stable family patterns generally associated with the middle class, and continue on to two interviewees whose lives took place in much poorer conditions, but their parents' valuation of education was crucial. To demonstrate clearly what was decisive for educational upward mobility in the core socialization group, I will focus on the parents' backgrounds, materially secure living conditions, and childhood lifestyles.

4.1.1   Parents' backgrounds as motors for children's educational upward mobility

Three factors in parents' backgrounds influenced their children's socialization toward educational upward mobility:

1. middle-class strands;
2. holding an exceptional position in their families; and
3. specific formative experiences.

I have described my rather formal approach to sample selection using the term *working class* mainly in alignment with the European Socio-economic Classification to facilitate comparisons. Now, my findings show that this categorization is very general, encompassing a wide range of educational backgrounds and occupations, some of which are very close to middle class. Thus, categorizing all the interviewees as members of the same social class as their parents is misleading, and their living conditions and lifestyles are, indeed, very diverse, ranging from security funded by decent civil service employment to precarious, below-poverty-threshold conditions. In this section, where socialization is found crucial for educational upward mobility, I will first describe the upper working-class families and come back to the lower working-class families later. For an overview of the interviewees, see Table 4.1.

In the first life history under study, a middle-class strand plays a crucial role. Eric Finch was born in 1964 and grew up in a suburban area in southern Essex. His mother left school at 16 and worked as a

Table 4.1 Interviewees whose parents' backgrounds were crucial for their educational upward mobility

Eric Finch (male)	born 1964	in England	Mother: compulsory school; secretary, manual worker in shoe and perfume factories (ESeC 9)
			Father: compulsory school; mill, kitchen, transport worker (ESeC 9)
Claudia Stangl (female)	born 1966	in Austria	Mother: compulsory school; housewife (ESeC 10)
			Father: skilled carpenter, civil servant in a carpentry in a jail (ESeC 8)
Stephanie Wollner (female)	born 1978	in Austria	Mother: compulsory school; cleaner (ESeC 9)
			Father: skilled carpenter; civil servant in a post office (ESeC 7)

secretary; later, she worked on the production line in a shoe factory and then a perfume factory. His father left school at 14 and got no further formal qualifications. He worked in a paper mill, moving from recycling to the pulping line to the production line until he was laid off and became first a kitchen and then a transport worker. Finch has a brother five years his senior and a sister two years older.

His mother is the key figure in his educational upward mobility. Her father, who was alive during Finch's upbringing, was a skilled engineer, clearly middle class, who had to stop working due to illness and moved socially downward. Finch notes that her middle-class youth 'instilled within my Mum a sense that you could do things differently'. It enabled her to envisage a wider range of possibilities. She went to school until she was 18 years old – later than the compulsory school-leaving age would have required – and participated in a secretarial course. Finch describes her as coming 'from a higher aspirational family' and identifies her as 'the key driving force, 'cos my Mum was the stronger of the two', referring to his father, a mill worker. His mother stood out in her own family for leaving social housing and moving away:

> My Mum was from a family of six or seven; my Dad was from a family of eight. I think. Eerm. They were the only, um, members of those family that didn't live in social housing. So they made a decision, I think, which is mainly directed by my Mum, that they

would buy their own home. So, in a sense of being slightly more upward mobile, they were there. And also interestingly, they were the only [pause] – um – apart from one of my Mum's sisters, they were the only ones that didn't – that moved out of the original home area, which was a place called T in E. They didn't go very far. It's only about 10–15 miles away. But in terms of the way the families viewed things, it was significantly different.

The decision to take a mortgage and leave social housing has huge meaning in the English context, as respectability is tightly connected to house ownership, and living in social housing is stigmatized. In addition, schools are generally better and more prestigious in wealthy areas than in poor residential areas, and, if they can afford to, parents move when their children become school-aged to ensure they attend certain schools. In fact, English universities consider from *which* school applicants received their certificate, which is not true in Austria. Compared with Austria and other German-speaking countries, then, England has a highly differentiated and hierarchical educational system from schools to universities.

Aspiration to material ownership goes along with changing location and is related to developing different views. This type of change is what Bourdieu means by the *'dialectic between interiority and exteriority ... between interiorisation of the exteriority and the exteriorisation of the interiority'* (2009, p. 164, emphasis original). Dynamically interrelated material conditions, values, attitudes, perceptions, and actions become 'structured structures'. Finch grew up in 'suburbia', playing with neighborhood kids in driveways without cars because 'all relied on public transport, went to the same schools largely'. I will come back to Finch's life history in Section 4.6 when I outline how gender affects educational upward mobility.

Another example of the influence of exceptional parents on educational upward mobility is Claudia Stangl. In her case, the father left his original family. His parents are farmers, and his brothers became unskilled workers, while he became a skilled carpenter. In addition, Stangl's maternal grandmother completed a secretarial course, and an uncle on her mother's side, who is only a couple of years older than Stangl, is the first in the family to go to university. Stangl describes her own way in relation to those of her cohort and her parents and grandparents:

First, my uncle finished because he also studied in the family, so he was a pioneer, and so, yes, on this family line, so, the children of his generation, they were able to benefit from educational opportunities. There were many who completed higher schools or graduated from university, but the parents and grandparents' generation did not have this opportunity. [5-second pause] We benefited from the educational policy of Kreisky in the 70s, there you go, otherwise it would not have been possible – for us, obviously not possible to go to a higher school or to uni because it would not have been possible financially.

Stangl's educational upward mobility is clearly embedded in the social welfare and educational expansion policy of the 1970s in Austria. This policy was characterized by the founding of many further leading schools, especially in rural areas. Stangl's upward mobility is also tightly connected to her maternal grandparents, who lived next door and had lived strands of a middle-class life, and to her father, who left his original family milieu to become a civil servant, working with inmates in a prison carpentry shop. I will come back to this point later. Stangl's upward mobility supports Bourdieu's emphasis on the stepwise process of change.

Stephanie Wollner's life demonstrates yet another dimension of the influence of parental background on educational upward mobility. She is the youngest of the sample, born in 1978 in upper Austria. She grew up in very secure and clearly structured circumstances. From age 10, she had guitar lessons, became very skillful, and went on to study guitar at a music university, but dropped out because she suffered from the competitive atmosphere and lack of recognition. She wanted to study social work but feared her father's disapproval.

For Wollner's educational upward mobility, her mother's formative experiences and their impact on the way she raised her daughters were crucial. Wollner's mother grew up on a farm with an older brother and a younger sister. Her parents decided that she would be the one to take over the farm once they became too old to maintain it, so at the end of compulsory schooling (nine years of schooling at that time) she started work in the hotel and restaurant industry. Her brother studied theology, a typical course for educationally upwardly mobile men in rural Austria, and her sister studied German language and literature. When Wollner's mother declared her wish to become a chemist's assistant, her mother fainted, a strategy she applied on other occasions as well to prevent something from happening. Wollner's mother felt ignorant and developed a strong wish that her own daughters would advance to higher education in whatever field they wished.

Once she became a mother, she worked in the mornings and evenings as a cleaner so that she could be at home when her daughters returned from school and see to their well-being as well as support and control their homework and preparation for exams. In Austria, school generally takes a half day, and children have a lot of homework. The school system is streamed after the four years of elementary school, which leads to an attitude shared by teachers and parents that pupils in the upper streams do not require teachers' support because they do not have to be there; their success is up to them or their parents. Consequently, parents provide immense support for their children to complete the upper streams successfully. When they cannot teach their children, a whole industry of private classes steps in (Arbeiterkammer Wien, 2013). Clearly, the Austrian school system reproduces social classes to a great extent.

The change in Wollner's life did not originate solely from her mother's upbringing, but also from the way she diverged from her parents' plan for her. She enrolled in two subjects, social economy and law, but actually studied only the former, without telling her father she was enrolled in it at all. Her subversive strategy was not restricted to her parents; she took long, looping paths to reach her original objective: to become a social worker. Her father dismissed this profession strongly, and, although her mother wanted to provide her daughter with greater freedom than she had, she did not oppose her husband's attitude but conveyed the message she absorbed when she was young: obey the father. Whatever 'new' her mother offered was framed by certain values, one of which holds that social work 'benefits scroungers'. Bourdieu says that the habitus is a principle of inventions and improvisations that take place within limits. Wollner studied social economy, the subject closest to her original wish, and, as an excellent student, was offered a job on a research project and later invited to work toward a PhD. She enjoyed studying, but suffered from the university's hierarchical and competitive structures and dropped out to have a child. After several trials in other occupations, she started working in social services and realized that she enjoyed it and wanted to continue.

Social change here is embedded partly in her parents' support, as in Finch's life, and partly in going against her parents' ideas and wishes. Social work is a subject traditionally studied by working-class people, many of whom enter the profession, so pursuing this path reflects limited social change. However, Wollner studied social economy and conducted research; her education differed from that of traditional social workers and enabled a wider view. This experience and her youthful music career reflect her aspiration to develop new concepts and pursue a different lifestyle from that of her parents, which continues social change.

4.1.2 Materially secure living conditions enabling a long perspective for upward educational mobility

I now turn to the material dimension of socialization that can lead to educational upward mobility. It is tied to middle-class culture in terms of the perceptions and attitudes discussed above. Six out of the eight life paths in which socialization was the crucial factor for upward mobility took place in a materially secure and relatively wealthy environment. Their parents' income allowed the interviewees to grow up in a certain lifestyle above the existential minimum and enabled them to gain a wider perspective on the world.

Table 4.2 Interviewees whose educational upward mobility stemmed from materially secure living conditions, in order of presentation

Scott Johnson (male)	born 1960	in England	Mother: compulsory school; cleaner (ESeC 9)
			Father: compulsory school; bank messenger (ESeC 9)
Eric Finch (male)	born 1964	in England	Mother: compulsory school; secretary, shoe and perfume factory worker (ESeC 9)
			Father: compulsory school; mill, kitchen, transport worker (ESeC 9)
Alexander Mair (male)	born 1966	in Austria	Parents' education and occupation unknown but in ESeC 7 at the highest
Claudia Stangl (female)	born 1966	in Austria	Mother: compulsory school; housewife (ESeC 10)
			Father: skilled carpenter, works as civil servant in a jail's carpentry shop (ESeC 8)
Stephanie Wollner (female)	born 1978	in Austria	Mother: compulsory school; cleaner (ESeC 9)
			Father: skilled carpenter, civil servant in a post office (ESeC 7)
Friedrich Schrieben (male)	born 1966	in Austria	Mother: skilled shop assistant, waitress (ESeC 9)
			Father: skilled metal worker, train driver (ESeC 8)

Scott Johnson's mother worked part-time as a cleaner in a Catholic church, which allowed the family to live in a house nearby, owned by the church. They enjoyed the status that generally goes along with owning a house, which, in England, defines the line between respectability and anything else in terms of social status. In Johnson's childhood, before the introduction of information technologies, his father worked as a bank messenger. He was extremely keen on education, for both his son and himself. He spent money on books and records, educational material goods that opened the world for Johnson.

> I suppose one thing [sigh] one thing I do remember when I was young is – with reference to education – there were always a lot of books in the house. Although my father was uneducated, he was, he was by no means stupid, if you know what I mean, and he was one of these people who – he placed a great value on education. I think, um, I know it's a terrible thing to say now, looking back on it, I sometimes think there was a sort of – in terms of his children and particularly myself – there was a sort of vicarious quality.

Johnson continued this sequence by explaining that he was his father's favorite child because he 'was probably the most academically able amongst us all, because none of the others actually went to, to tertiary education'. How his father's extraordinary appreciation of education became crucial for Johnson, I will explain in more detail later in Section 4.1.3 on lifestyle.

Another example of material conditions that broaden horizons and contribute to a wider perspective are holidays, which enable people to see other parts of the country or even other countries: 'So that [the financial situation] actually made things much more sensible, and much more livable, workable. We had a summer holiday every year – two weeks away', Eric Finch said. His father worked as an unskilled mill worker until Eric was at the end of the sixth form in college, when his father was laid off, increasing Eric's politicization and influencing his decision to go to university. Finch's mother (coming from a middle-class family, as outlined in the previous section) worked as a secretary, and later in a shoe factory and thereafter in a perfume factory on the production line. Both of his parents' salaries together allowed the family of five to live in a semi-detached bungalow with an extra room they built in the attic after obtaining a planning permit.

Alexander Mair was nine years old when he, his parents, and his younger brother first went away on holiday. 'We were then travelling to Tirol on holidays for the following years, to hike.' The father worked for a company with its main branch in Tirol, so they stayed in a bed-and-breakfast run by his father's colleague. His mother worked part-time, and this family owned a house. Mair also appreciated the new clothes they bought him: 'I have always been quite well off, so it was [laughs], we always had a lot, I don't know what, ah, for example, clothes, we always had new clothes, so this was, it was actually, quite comfortable.' His parents were members of a savings club and met with other members every two weeks on Saturdays. Mair was not eligible for a study grant because his parents earned too much.

Two interviewees' fathers were civil servants. Claudia Stangl's father was a carpenter working at a prison. Her mother was a housewife. They, too, went on holidays, even abroad: 'Yes, holidays were important for us kids. We travelled somewhere within Austria and also to Croatia, to the seaside. These were common activities, with our immediate family, but also together with our grandparents, so there were common holidays and common activities.'

They built a house together with the neighbors' support in the round-robin way typical of 1960s rural Austria. In Stangl's case, her father's income brought an abundance of concrete experiences; the children were allowed to take part in the house building by experimenting with different materials, which made a strong impression on Stangl's way of learning and interests.

Wollner's father was also a carpenter but, at 20, went to work in a post office and kept the position until he retired. Compared with England, Austria still has a strong culture of civil service positions, which enable even lower-income families to develop the long-term perspective crucial for developing aspirations, while providing a material basis for participation in higher education. In both families, the parents worked in jobs below tertiary professional education while developing a clear plan for their children to graduate from universities and to become professionals. While Wollner was in elementary school, she wanted to learn to play the guitar. She had a neighbor, ten years older than she was, whom she admired very much. Her parents were able to pay for her private music lessons and, as their daughter was very talented, to send her to a private music-focused school affiliated with a music university, smoothing her path into the highly competitive field of music study. The private secondary school also offered a general school-leaving certificate that was accepted for entrance to other universities. It required a monthly fee and Wollner also had a very good, very costly instrument: 'And I believe they actually invested a lot. The school was private. It charged fees. Hmm, I don't know, I believe at the end, this was about 1,000 Schillings per term. So, was actually, I believe, relatively a lot of money for my parents. [incomprehensible] Self-made, hand-made guitar, it cost 40,000 Schillings in these days.' The point here is that, without her parents' income, Wollner would not have had the enriching experience of learning to play an instrument almost professionally, something that broadened her horizons immensely and took her into a world beyond the one she grew up in.

Another interviewee's parents earned enough to pay for his private music lessons. Friedrich Schrieben's father was a skilled metal worker and drove trains; his mother was a skilled shop assistant and worked as a waitress. His uncle led a brass band in a small town, and Schrieben started to play the flute when he was five years old. He had clarinet lessons later and, as a teenager, played in a big band; at university, he earned extra money playing in his own band. Music played a crucial role in his life, both as an enriching experience and as a source of money. When he went to lower secondary school (ISCED 2), he experienced a lot of pressure, and his parents paid for private classes to help him to succeed:

> naturally, you always grappled and always learned too little and always hoped you wouldn't be called on and so there was the constant pressure not to fail, was naturally constant, always there, because basically you – almost everyone stayed back a year, and you had tests and homework, so it was – when you were always at the limit somehow, it was natural that you said, ok, the pressure is enormous, I need to say this, at which, as I said [5-second pause], my parents never punished me on anything, naturally they paid for private lessons for me, so that when I was in grade 7 and had the two English and French problems, no, there was no question about it.

In Austria, every subject must be passed in order to proceed; otherwise, pupils must repeat the whole year. In this context, the pressure Schrieben describes and the huge market for private classes are comprehensible. Educational progress can depend directly on money. This quote demonstrates that his underperformance was due to lack of preparation for tests, and that his parents did not hesitate but paid for private classes as a matter of course. A similar situation occurred when Schrieben took much longer to complete his university studies than the full grant he received allowed. By then, his father was annoyed, but his mother and grandmother provided him with money: 'and naturally my granny, whom I also repeatedly, every week that went by, visited and then again and again she gave me a hundred or rather five hundred, so there was that – and naturally my parents, well, my mother, like my granny, an angel of generosity, always had money somehow'.

Overall, this section relates to the upper spheres of the working class, with Wollner's father at the top in terms of ESeC 7. It is also apparent that materially secure living conditions were linked to a historical period in which the welfare state became strong, even in England.

4.1.3 Childhood lifestyle: a loving atmosphere enabling educational development

Closely connected to materially secure living conditions is a certain childhood lifestyle that the same six interviewees I listed at the beginning of the last section experienced. The literature review on educational upward mobility pointed to the importance of parental support for children's educational success. Among the people I interviewed, I also found mainly mothers helping their children with homework and other tasks, but an especially enabling context was created by parents who loved their children in such a way that the children felt free and not under pressure. The most important and enabling circumstance for educational upward mobility in terms of children's lifestyle were loving, caring, and present parents. Certain related values were crucial. A common feature in the lives of five interviewees was high consistency, which I will describe below. A supportive aspect was the environment in which the family life was embedded offering possibilities for material and emotional support. Last, but not least, external stimulation, such as the private music classes I have mentioned, strongly affected childhood lifestyles. I will start with the emotional ways in which parents nurtured their children and interlace the other aspects. This section will clarify the abstract notion of habitus with real-life examples.

I will start with the oldest interviewee in this group. Johnson was born in 1960, when England's welfare state and higher education system were quite strong and expanding. His closeness to his father was crucial for his educational upward mobility. The core of their relationship, educational activities, built on his father's very strong valuation of education, while his mother was more important in providing comfort and did not play a crucial role in educational activities or decisions. Generally speaking, Johnson should not have succeeded in education because of his working-class background, but his father was so eager for him to succeed and provided such good conditions for him to succeed that it would have been surprising if he had *not* earned a degree. On the other hand, he is the only one of his three siblings who participated in higher education. The crucial question is why? One answer might be that he was the most *able*. He admitted to a talent for maths and sciences, and he did well in other subjects, so, in general, he was academically very good. He also *studied a lot*, deployed effort, while his younger brother did not study and decided against university, although he went through his A levels. The youngest brother did not pass his A levels easily, but only with so much pressure from his father that the son's hair fell out.

Let's look more closely at the strong appreciation for education embedded in secure material living conditions that formed Johnson's disposition and organized his practices. The starting point was his father's own hunger for education. When Johnson was in grammar school, his father went to evening classes to study maths, and Johnson helped him with his homework. Later, they discussed evolution:

> He cared a lot about my education it felt; he really valued it, which is why I said something about it being almost vicarious – that because he hadn't had the opportunities [sigh] [pause], he was – I'm not – I don't know if my father was ever going to be capable or ever would have been capable – it's very hard to tell because you didn't know him when he was younger, of course. I

think – because you've not received that education when you're younger, of course…but he, he did want to know things. He wanted to know things until they were contrary to the Bible then he got a bit funny, but [laughs] he was – we had some very interesting discussions on [laughs], um, evolution was a good one, we used to do that, and you know, age of the universe. So he was, um [pause], yeah, he was quite happy to, to learn things. And he had quite a logical mind.

Johnson's father was intrinsically engaged in education, which infected Johnson and provided him with opportunities to become educated. The new came into his life through his father, who was vivid, vocal, and active, with many different interests and hobbies. His father was a steady man, too, fulfilling the role of the patriarch, but always bringing something new to life and being open-minded. Education was one of the new elements the father brought into the family when he went to evening classes and studied maths, when he played chess with his son, when he bought an encyclopedia to bring knowledge into the little house, when he wanted to discuss topics that go against the Church with his son. The father provided space for development. He was authoritarian, but let the son decide and grow and live his own life.

Johnson's own engagement was rewarded at school with praise and good marks, which encouraged him to continue. His educational upward mobility was characterized by a dynamic of positively reinforcing engagement ('I always enjoyed learning from, from day one. I was quite studious I think as a child'), effort during A levels ('I used to work in the kitchen…my parents were quite good about that…and work until 11 o'clock at night'), and success in terms of good marks and the affirmation of teachers. Despite the father's high appreciation of education, it was not self-evident that Johnson would continue in school, and he had to negotiate with his parents, who insisted that he get a Saturday job when he went off to stay at school. He had to keep the job until exams, when his parents gave him pocket money from money he had given them earlier. After Johnson completed four A levels (three are the standard), his parents' attitude changed. Their alteration was embedded in the material conditions of the time, when lower-income parents could rely on welfare state funding for their children's studies:

I applied to university, this sort of – it also seemed to follow you were supposed to do this, there was no real consideration about whether to go to university or not because I'd got to this stage, and it was just, it just seemed assumed – even by my parents – that this was next. And I think – there was some sort of kudos for my father in this: My son is going off to university [laughs], sorry, a bit of reminiscence there. And he – because we were not wealthy, it wasn't going to cost him anything, the fact I went to university anyway; I would be living at home, and in those days you got grants; there was no student loans or anything, so I got a full – I qualified for a full maintenance grant.

This quote illustrates how the self-evidence of going to university is tightly linked to material conditions that enable it and the educationally positive attitude of parents.

Social change takes a long time. In this case, it started with the father, and the son realized his capacity very slowly, with forward and backward steps. Although Johnson finished his A levels, he did not acquire a university degree straight away. He applied to Oxford and spent the night before the interview in a college. He said that the bathroom was bigger than his whole house, and he felt totally overwhelmed. By the time he got to the interview, he was a nervous wreck, and it went badly.

He applied to other universities and finally went to University College London, where he began studying electrical engineering, an applied subject, despite his interest in pure mathematics. His maths teacher had argued that there was no money in maths. Johnson received a full maintenance grant and got jobs in the summer. After a year, he realized that he was studying the wrong subject. He had to leave the students' dorm but could not afford a flat in London, so he moved out of the city. He struggled through his second year, lost contact with fellow students, and failed in the third. In 1980, at the age of 20, he dropped out.

He worked in an electronics shop for the next 20 years. He married and fathered two children. His job was not demanding, and he enrolled in the Open University, where he enjoyed studying and made faster progress than other part-timers. His third child was born; his company rationalized; and his work increased without any increase in remuneration. Johnson's line manager had a breakdown, and Johnson took over his shifts in addition to his own. His father died. Overworked, Johnson grew severely depressed and was released. The following year, his mother died, leaving him £80,000. The money enabled him to study again. He finished his degree at the Open University and continued at another university until he became ill. He ran out of money but, after recovering, received a small student loan and finished his BSc. At the time of the interview, he was working on his PhD in general relativity in a program that allowed him to skip his Master's, and he had a grant. He was in his mid-fifties and did not aspire to a university career, but was interested in teacher training.

Johnson is the only one of his siblings who picked up on the new his father brought home, but the related social change took decades. His educational upward mobility was a long and winding road, with long interruptions. Ensuring material existence came first and studying second, as a kind of luxury, even when paid for by the state. Working-class culture was strong in this family, and Johnson kept his connection to it by doing his A Levels *and* working. He could accommodate this compromise because he was not only able but hard-working, studying until late at night. Adhering at least partly to the family culture was necessary to start something new. Note that studying for Johnson was based not only on material security but also on joy. He did not consider it a means to an end – employability – as Lehmann (2008) claims for a sample of first-generation students at a Canadian university. Johnson seemed to make a rather middle-class demand on study: it must be satisfying in itself. He might have picked up this criterion early from his father, who was purely. intrinsically interested in education, and it might reflect an earlier change in mindset, preceding more material social change, demonstrating the overall dynamic of his upward mobility.

Let us now examine a different lifestyle and way of enabling educational upward mobility. Eric Finch, who belongs to one of the materially secure families discussed in the previous section, described his parents' love as unconditional, so he grew up in an emotionally secure context as well. A sequence in which he described his parents' reaction to his wish to go to university makes it clear that their unconditional love had a twofold impact. It enabled the parents to let their son go and the son to go, because both sides were confident that going to university was not too great a risk: 'Um – and I think they also understood that – you know, whatever happened, I would be all right. I'd always have the fall back on them if anything went terribly wrong.' In Bourdieu's theoretical framework, his parents' love could be interpreted as a principle that generated and organized practices: here, the confidence to start something new.

Finch's family life had an exceptional feature: his father worked mostly night shifts and was usually at home when the children returned from school, preparing tea and doing most of the cooking. He would be sleeping when the children left and awake in the afternoons, when their mother was at her secretarial job. Despite this untraditional division of labor at home, Finch grew up in a social context of strong gender hierarchies in which higher education was reserved for men. This value structure was decisive for his educational upward mobility because he was the 'right' gender, and his 'academically bright, very bright' sister was not. I will focus on this point later.

A strong feature of his family's lifestyle was regular meals:

> then home in the evening, a bit of homework, although I was always very late into doing homework, er, a bit of playing, and we would all sit together and eat tea together, and the only time when that started stopping was when my brother went to, um, sixth form college. Uum [pause]. Actually [pause], did that change? It didn't even change then. I think my brother left school at 16 and started working, and I think that's when it started stopping being us all eating a meal together. Um, we all sat round the table to have our meal, and that was on Thursday nights, because we would have fresh bread and jam and something else. And that was the only time we were allowed not to eat together at the table. Every other time we ate together at the table.

No clear, direct connection has been established between regular family meals and educational upward mobility. Nevertheless, regularity, continuity, the absence of change in terms of moving or a parental separation is a feature I found in four of the five families in this group.

Apart from his father often being at home in the afternoons, Finch's childhood was very similar to those around him. His neighborhood was very homogeneous – people owned houses but not cars, so the driveways were free for play. Children went to the same school on public transport and felt safe and without pressure in terms of anxiety or competition.

Friedrich Schrieben's father was also often at home in the afternoons. He drove a train, and every 35 days his shift changed, and when he finished his morning shift he came home at two o'clock in the afternoon. Both parents provided loving care in this family, but in very different ways. While his mother was cheerful, his father was driven to promote and stimulate his sons. 'For him, it was naturally understood that there would no limitation in whatever form concerning the education of the children; that is, anything we wanted to do was – it was, with him, it was always: "Dare to do something!" '

Schrieben's father was a metal worker, a profession that demands accuracy to tenths of millimeters, and, as a train driver, accuracy was required to protect passengers. Schrieben presented his father as suffering from this accuracy; a cupboard hanging askew reminded him of the abundance of imprecision in his environment. He was the oldest son, and his parents told him to be responsible. As a result, he wanted his own sons to have freedom:

'he wished that his children would be a bit more open; that is, he would have loved to find in his children everything he was not, so that they would have fun, they would be able to chat, and they would be able to entertain a circle, which perhaps he wasn't able to, he would have liked, and yes, that was then, I was a very carefree child'.

Parents' backgrounds strongly influence the formative experiences crucial for their children's educational upward mobility. In Schrieben's case, his father gave his son the leeway to develop at his own pace in accordance with his own needs, although he became impatient when Schrieben's studies took seven years.

Schrieben's father had many interests, such as beekeeping. He played tennis with his son, a sport of the middle classes in 1970s Austria. The other, more important external stimulation Schrieben's parents provided was the private music lessons.

Alexander Mair grew up in a loving atmosphere that extended to his maternal grandparents, who lived about 300 meters away. 'It was very loving at home, both with my parents and with my grandparents.' When I asked for a concrete example of this atmosphere, he paused for five seconds and replied, 'Concrete situation – it is, was simply, generally, there was a great backing, that is – that is – yes, also with p – also very much praise, and yes, so that was very comfortable'. I asked, 'From both parents'? and he answered, 'Yes. Perhaps a little more from mum.'

Mair received very good marks at school, and his parents encouraged him to continue and not to take an apprenticeship. As in Finch's case, the love and care of Mair's parents seemed to open space for development without a fixed destination but oriented toward Mair's specific needs, as shown in the following exchange:

> *AM*: Yes, that is actually, it was never actually pressed upon me: you must to go on, you know, but [5-second pause] I simply imagined it for myself, yes, I'd prefer if I would, if I would learn more and would not start an apprenticeship or anything like that now [5-second pause]. So, yes, I don't know now whether it was 100 per cent my own decision, but it was simply, yes [laughs].
>
> *AK*: Yes, your parents, is – ? You wanted to continue, and your parents agreed?
>
> *AM*: It was OK, that, yes.
>
> *AK*: Your brother preferred to do an apprenticeship?
>
> *AM*: Yes, that was definitely his idea, inasmuch as he said, finish school as fast as possible [laughs] and learn something and yes.
>
> *AK*: And how did your parents react?
>
> *AM*: That was also OK.

No conscious steering toward something special or concrete, such as a certain professional career, characterized the parents' education of their sons. Rather, their caring functioned as an invisible structuring structure, giving both sons the space to develop their interests and to choose their professions.

Stability in Mair's life is manifest predominantly in the long-term continuities that characterized his education. He grew up in a small town in upper Austria where he went to elementary school and from grades five to eight to *Hauptschule*, which is the lower of two types of streamed schools (ISCED 254), but often the highest level in rural areas that lack *Gymnasien*. At *Hauptschule*, his teacher had been his father's teacher. From grades eight to thirteen, Mair went to an upper vocational school (ISCED 354) that offered the highest school-leaving degree, the prerequisite for university-level study. There, he studied mechanical technology for five years with one teacher, who encouraged Mair and his classmates to study at the technical university where he had studied. With five classmates, Mair travelled the 200 kilometers to check out the dormitories. He decided to attend and shared a dorm room with two former classmates. Mair's educational upward mobility generated and organized practices that embedded his university education in his original milieu, so he could move up step by step without alienation. 'Next step was the course in L, so, as I already mentioned, the catalyst was my teacher K [laughs], and yes I must say in hindsight, thank God [laughs]. I never regretted it, so that was, that, I think, yes, thank God he did that so – did so much propaganda and portrayed it so positively.'

At this small technical university, the 50-student class allowed close contact with members of staff and a familial atmosphere. What was new in Mair's life was embedded in the familiar, so his educational upward mobility can be compared to spinning the same thread with new wool. His habitus is to search what he knows, to secure himself, to run no risk.

Claudia Stangl also grew up in a nurturing environment. She describes her parents' reaction to the good marks she received at school:

CS: There was actually no question about that as the marks were always good – As and Bs, there was no question. They did not fuss about it since they were good, it was not, not so important.

AK: Then praise or something – ?

CS: Praise for good results, yes, all right, but not the way – you need to get a lot of As – and like that, but they simply appreciated the performance and the work and always made sure that I could study in a quiet atmosphere, so especially to take on additional workloads, or yes, they had a lot of respect for that.

Stangl's mother expressed her caring concretely by helping her daughter focus on her homework. This practice led to the daughter's disposition to carry out the tasks she received from school without questioning or forgetting or failing and on her own, but not alone, as she worked in her mother's presence:

> So, my mother always made sure whether we had homework, whether there was something she could help with, yes, she had an eye on that, but I did my homework very rapidly, very autonomously, my homework, and I had always a central place, sitting in the kitchen, yes, yes, and there I did my homework, and this was rather the main place, where my mother was. So, she always realized which things needed to be done or not. Contact with the school took place on parents' days here and there, I don't remember anymore precisely how this was with parents' meetings in the elementary school, so the usual, anticipated contact was handled by my mother. My father was not involved in that so much. Mainly, when he came home, the topic of school was already finished; we had begun our leisure time.

While Stangl's mother created the optimal conditions for school success, her father offered a learning environment apart from school. He ran a carpentry workshop at home and allowed her to help, and she learned quite a lot. Her relationship with her father focused on practical projects; they built a fish pond together, for example.

In several of the close families that characterize this group, grandparents lived close by or in the same house and played a crucial role. Stephanie Wollner's family lived with her grandparents because her mother was the sibling designated to take over care of the farm. Claudia Stangl lived her first years at her grandparents' house until the house her parents were building close by was ready. Her maternal grandfather was a railwayman, a profession traditionally occupied by Social Democrats in Austria. He was also a Protestant, a minority group in mainly Catholic Austria that often represented progress in contrast to tradition. Family values from her mother's side dominated the conservative values of her father's side because the maternal grandparents lived so close by. The household's mixture of closeness and freedom to develop can be attributed to the grandfather.

In contrast, her father's family was shaped by rural peasant structures and the conservative policies embodied by her uncle, who was borough counsellor of the Austrian Peoples' Party (*Österreichische Volkspartei*, ÖVP). At home, Stangl and her parents discussed controversial policies and sometimes did not understand each other, 'but at least there was a mutual respect so that, not so, so that nobody was expelled from home. It is simply – the opinion of the other person is simply accepted, and that was mutual. I always knew that I would not be able to change the basic opinions of my father or my mother, so somehow the mutual respect was actually continuous – was there on both sides.'

To understand how this value structure of basic openness to let the children develop on their own enabled Stangl's educational upward mobility, we must go back a step in her biography. During elementary school, a neighbor invited her to participate in Friends of Children (*Kinderfreunde*), an organization funded privately at the beginning of the twentieth century and shortly thereafter integrated with, and run by, the Social Democrats in Austria. The neighbor was a chemist from the German Democratic Republic, who had a son a couple of years older than Stangl, and who organized a Friends of Children group in a small town two kilometers away. She asked Stangl's parents if she could take their daughter to these weekly meetings, lasting about an hour and a half. Stangl's parents agreed. The children hiked and attended events and workshops and, during holidays, camps. Stangl described her neighbor and the activities as follows:

Yes, she was a bit, she had – she came from East Germany, and she spoke German – this was interesting and made us curious – she was a bit different from others and therefore woke our curiosity and actually also this – So she led these group meetings and made them interesting, and there was always something new, so we, for us kids always, so, as I just said, for example developing photos, stuff that made us curious and was a bit exotic and woke our interests and also our curiosity, so that we always went there or went with her and participated. This was certainly also very much connected to the person, and she contacted kids to join the group and she led the group. And for her also the scientific stuff and nature, to be outdoors in natural surroundings, was important, this fitted well with my interests, and for example, she knew an incredible number of names of plants and introduced many things that interested me a lot.

Apart from these inspiring and stimulating weekly activities that broadened Stangl's horizons, experience, and knowledge, Stangl had contact with this woman and her son as neighbors.

As a neighbor, I always had contact because she had a child, a son, a couple of years older than me, but lived close by, and we played together, and so we came into this family's home from time to time and met her there often. And that was fascinating because it was the only house that had a swimming pool and that was naturally also very great for us kids, that we could use this swimming pool, and I remember that they had rings hanging in their living room, that was fascinating for us kids to be allowed to play directly in the room, so a little bit a – she brought a little bit of a different life into the village. She was smiled at sometimes, but that – but that made us kids certainly very curious.

This contact enabled her to get to know another way of living, unfamiliar but tolerated by her family, so she was able to enjoy the experience. The opportunity was deeply linked to her family's social status and political value structure as working class, not farmers. The following quote illustrates this point. I had asked her whether her friends also joined Friends of Children.

Well, they were naturally more farmers' kids; they tended to not be allowed to go there because Friends of Children were then politically more, certainly even more than now categorized politically. They did not go there, the rural neighbors, but friends from housing estates, working-class kids, I met them there, so from school, from elementary school, and students from the *Hauptschule* went there, I believe a neighbor from a farm went once for a while to group meetings and also my sister, she also participated, she also went along on the trips, joined.

Friends of Children played a crucial role throughout Stangl's life. When she was 15, she joined the Red Falcons, the organization's venue for teenagers, and became a leader of a children's group. At 19, she joined the peace movement and had contentious political discussions with her parents. She became a Red Falcons representative at the district and county levels during her university studies. After ten years of employment in different educational organizations, she became the director of a Friends of Children camp and was still working there at the time of the interview. She ran programs very similar to the one she had experienced, closely related to nature and science, working with many materials, and practically oriented.

In regard to social change, Stangl did not lead the same life as her parents. As in many migrant families, Stangl's parents represent a transition from a traditional to a modern lifestyle. Her father enjoyed his profession, and her mother seemed content with her work at home. Stangl grew up in the countryside, but her family structure was not peasant. Her paternal grandparents were farmers, conservatives, voting for the *Österreichische Volkspartei*, but her maternal grandparents, with whom she lived and grew up, were workers, left-wing, and Protestants. Her maternal grandmother had secretarial training and was briefly employed. Her parents consciously desired and supported the new in Stangl's life. The new was embedded in her family and her milieu and closely tied to her class and time, the 1970s, with Kreisky's social-democratic and welfare-oriented policies reflected in Stangl's engagement in social-democratic child and youth organizations, the peace movement, the newly funded school, and her professional career.

Stephanie Wollner experienced a much more controlling style of care. Her mother actively trained her daughter, checking samples of her homework and making her perform: for example, prompting her to produce English vocabulary. The mother kept in close contact with Wollner's teachers beyond the regularly scheduled parents' evenings. For example, when Wollner failed her first Italian homework assignment and became desperate because of her bad mark, the mother spoke with the teacher, who offered to allow Wollner to take the exam after the class was over, so she would not be obliged to compare it with the other students'. Further, if this strategy did not work, she said she would think of another. However, her lenience was enough security for Wollner, and she performed well.

Overall, the lifestyles described in this section may come as a surprise in their resemblance to a more middle-class stereotype. Loving, caring, respectful, and supportive child-rearing may depend on secure material living conditions. Blaming working-class parents for not educating their children without looking at their material living conditions is putting the cart before the horse. Welfare state benefits, among other material resources and time, are essential to building loving, reliable, and effective childcare.

4.1.4 Poor material conditions and affinity for education

Most of the educationally upwardly mobile interviewees who grew up in materially secure conditions were born in the 1960s. For two interviewees born in the 1930s, socialization was also crucial for upward educational mobility but embedded in very poor living conditions.

Gerhard Moser grew up in the lower strata of working-class families in a town where he, his parents, and two siblings lived in a flat consisting of a kitchen and one room without water or toilet. Their main food was corn, with potatoes and other vegetables from their garden. His primary school had one classroom for pupils of various ages, a slate, and a sponge. When he was nine or ten years old, his father got a job in industry in a city, and the family's living conditions improved considerably, but they were still very poor. From then on, the family lived in a 'flat with kitchen, room[s], closet, and above all, bathroom and toilet', Moser said.

He was raised during the National Socialist dictatorship, a period of modernization and improvement of material conditions, but, in contrast to the majority, Moser's parents did not become Nazis. Moser was selected and fully equipped with clothes and a ticket to Bohemia

Table 4.3 Interviewees who grew up in poor living conditions whose socialization was educationally affirmative

Gerhard Moser (male)	born in 1931	in Austria	Mother: no information on her education; day laborer (ESeC 9)
			Father: skilled miller, miner, steel worker (ISCED 453; ESeC 9)
Erwin Radler (male)	born in 1939	in Austria	Mother: compulsory school; household help, industrial worker (ESeC 9)
			Father: skilled scythe smith; partly captive (ISCED 453; ESeC 8 and temporarily 10)

to attend an elite boarding school for future Nazi leaders, when his mother intervened. Both parents were confirmed Catholics, to whom living their religion entailed providing loving socialization to their children; a very important dimension was education. Both came from extremely poor and desperate living conditions in what is now Slovenia. His mother maintained her siblings after her father died in the First World War and her mother died shortly after. Moser's father was raised by a foster family; he stayed with his mother for only a short time and never knew his father. When Moser was born, nine years after his sister, his parents had improved their living standard.

> Because they came from the poorest conditions, and they realized that it is possible to get on if one has the right education, so for them, school education was one of the utmost concerns from the beginning, even though they had no chance to have it themselves. And now they encouraged us to do it, and we picked up and accomplished it, so your own determination – that is the decisive there, that is what it comes down to, either I want to or I don't; no, if you have a goal then you need to go for it, otherwise you'll never achieve it. ... we had a very good relationship with our parents, they were very loving parents, yes, but they could only give us what they had in them, what was possible. But, please, perhaps that is also explainable, because my parents were very religious, yes and that they also received this impetus from religion, yes, that must – so this love must be given to the children. That is right, that explains it, no?

Clearly, his parents' love and care did not come out of the blue but were developed as they and their lifestyle developed. Their values work as a structuring structure for Moser:

> Oh, well, my parents were busy, yes, as I said, father in the mine in R, mother in the brickworks, and so I was then in school, and when we came home, we were on our own, work, homework, I basically always did on my own, yes, support from my parents was there, ideally support existed naturally, that they said: 'yes, you must be hard-working, you must see that you get ahead', so this was there massively from both of them, but they could not help me because they had no school education.

The religious element in Moser's education provided concrete opportunities. He was engaged in the congregation and became a youth group leader, Later, he served an apprenticeship with a Catholic publisher and secured a position there.

When Moser learned about the evening school that offered him a second chance to obtain the highest school-leaving degree, providing access to universities in almost all subjects but the arts, is not clear. However, he knew about it quite early and planned to reach higher education through this mechanism. He went on to study agriculture at a small university where he enjoyed the close atmosphere. Afterward, he worked for two years as a research fellow there and then moved to the Ministry of Agriculture and a career as civil servant.

The new in his life started with his apprenticeship because it led, not to a future in publishing, but to the evening school. The new was also related to his experiences; perhaps he chose to study agriculture as a result of the hunger he suffered after the war, and his employment as a civil servant was a way to avoid his father's experience of being laid off when the mill burned down and remaining unemployed.

At the same time, Moser's life history is another example of educational upward mobility perceived as the self-evident 'thing to do'. Look at his sister's educational career: she was nine years older than he and dead at the time of the interview. Born in 1922, she obtained the highest school-leaving degree, went to Vienna, studied economics, and earned a PhD. She emigrated to Canada and later Australia, and Moser lost touch with her. He did not say a lot about her, attributing his silence to faulty memory and her being much older, but I had the impression that he did not see her life history as exceptional. *This* appraisal surprises me and adds to the impression that higher education was the self-evident way to go in his family, but I cannot substantiate it from the interview text.

Erwin Radler is another instance in which socialization played a crucial role for educational upward mobility in a poor family. In contrast to his parents, Radler did not estimate education highly, but saw it as an escape from work. Nevertheless, other family values were crucial.

Radler was born when his mother was 22, and her highest educational level was compulsory school. She came from a small village in upper Austria. His father was from a town in upper Austria, 35 years old, and a scythe smith. Radler had a brother one year his senior who became a carpenter and foreman and died in 1978. When Radler was three, his first sister was born. She finished compulsory school and worked as household help and an industrial worker. When Radler was five, another sister was born, who became a certified nurse.

Radler's father was a convinced National Socialist. After the war, when Radler was six, his father was detained on political grounds for two years in Glasenbach. Later, he had to pay a fine due to political activities that were not clearly defined in the interview. Radler said this fine impoverished them:

> my father was a National Socialist and [held] this peculiar view: I have never done anything I did not think was right; therefore I do need not to deny anything, and if today they believe that was wrong, then let them punish me. That was his opinion, so he – he actually did not have a high income – we were four kids – by itself my father's income would have been sufficient to live on, but because he also had to pay a fine and so we had, my whole childhood, only the existential minimum. I can't remember anything apart from the bare minimum and for example what others had – extra vacation pay or Christmas bonus – my father used that to pay the fine and then had – my father worked every weekend so that we wouldn't want for anything, and the clothing, that was then practically – that was not affordable because everything my father had to spare we spent on food for the family, clothing – it went so far that we went carolling and what came out of it was a meter of cloth for long trousers – those were my first long trousers – we had in winter only short trousers with stockings, and those were our first long trousers – my brother and I earned them by carolling.

His mother was Catholic and very religious. At home, high ethical values prevailed: effort, honesty, and courage. Radler had a strong disposition to apply effort, to be resilient, honest, true to himself, never to live at others' expense but to contribute to the community, and, finally, to be respected and recognized.

He grew up in a milieu of scythe smiths, both socially and professionally. A neighbor, the wife of an old smith, taught Radler to read before he went to school. His parents did not know. In compulsory school, a teacher asked him to help to fix teaching materials and gave him books as a reward. He still had these books at the time of the interview. The smithy had a library, and he read not only Karl May but also nonfiction. In fourth grade, his seat-mate, son of a community secretary (*Gemeindesekretär*), had to prepare for admission to the *Gymnasium* (upper secondary school, ISCED 344), and, to help, Radler learned with him. 'And then I planned to learn Latin once', he remembered when he eventually started evening school.

After compulsory school, he had difficulty obtaining an apprenticeship, so he started work in the scythe smithy. At the age of 18, he began an apprenticeship as a metal tool maker with the same company. Here, he found an example in his master craftsman:

> the second key experience for me, even though I was always curious, was my master craftsman in the apprenticeship. People said of him 'the harder he works, the happier he is', which means the more difficult something is, the greater is his joy, and I never once heard him say 'we can't do this', yes, the most he said was 'yes, we need to try and see', no, and he eagerly took on things he did not know, so he gave me an example that you should not fear something unknown but face it, and that was the most important, actually.

During this time, he enrolled in, and paid for, distance-learning courses on metal working in machine building. In his final year at the vocational school, his class teacher and the subject teacher gave him permission to miss exams to meet orders for products.

> in the early mornings I went to the workshop to fill orders; for example molds and tools for... and it went so far that I told my class teacher, for example, today I can't because I do have an exam in accountancy. He asked, Did you study? I said yes. Then we went to the accountancy teacher, and the class teacher said, I need him today, and she said, Do you know the material? and I said yes. And then I went to the workshop.

In 1957, following his apprenticeship, he enrolled in the evening school and lived in the *Kolpinghaus*, a very cheap home for craftsmen, while working full-time, which was then 48 hours a week. From March 1958 until he completed evening school, Radler stopped working to complete his obligatory military service. After basic training, he took a course to become a corporal and train soldiers. The precondition for continuing his studies in the evening was to be the best in his unit.

After earning the highest school-leaving degree, he moved to another city to study technical physics. He received study grants from several foundations and, later, official state funding for students of parents with low incomes. He married and fathered two sons. In 1967, he completed his studies with distinction. He started a career with a company, then started his own business and taught part-time at an upper vocational technical school. After his wife died, he worked full-time at the vocational school and engaged in various community projects, such as exhibitions. A myocardial infarction led him to retire at the age of 60.

Socialization was crucial for Radler's educational upward mobility. The family value of effort led him to perform excellently throughout his educational and professional life. Both his mother and father were hard-working; his mother maintained a family of five while his father was detained, and his father worked extra hours to pay the fine. Obviously, Radler was also highly gifted, but, from early childhood on, he actively sought education and applied huge effort to receive it. He learned to read before attending school; he read the books in the smithy library; he studied to support his classmate's access to the *Gymnasium*; he enrolled in distance learning during his apprenticeship and studied his vocational school subjects as well; he went to evening school while working and used military achievement to be allowed to continue evening school. He sought grants when he went to university and studied hard to complete all his subjects in the shortest possible time. His socialization created the resilience that helped him to succeed despite the odds. He grew up in a milieu where authorities were highly respected – his father, his teachers, his master craftsman – and his respect enabled him to learn from them: 'To me, it was obvious that I wanted to learn from the teacher and that he would not adjust to me, but I must adjust to him. That was always obvious to me; that's why I never had any problems with a teacher because I simply said, So what? I'm learning for myself and not for the teacher.'

In his rural milieu, practical competence and work were required and central. Identities were created through activities, occupations, and knowledge. Consequently, Radler sought opportunities to be active and to enhance his knowledge, which brought him to new competencies and knowledge. Twice in the interview, he mentioned that his father was ashamed of him for studying and not working; his father considered him a laggard for going to university. It is somehow tragic that his father contributed so much to his son's educational upward mobility, yet could not appreciate it and even felt ashamed of his success. What enabled Radler to find studying and higher education an area worth investing effort in is not clear, especially when his father held strictly to the workplace as the proper arena to apply this highly estimated value. However, without the value of effort inculcated from early childhood as his habitus, Radler would not have been educationally upwardly mobile.

In terms of socialization, we find no fundamental differences between Austria and England. Education-enabling socialization seems to occur on a level that is not linked to, or dependent on, country-specific features but takes place in a more general dimension.

4.2   Change in objective structures

Bourdieu mentions change of objective structures as a possible motor for change of habitus. One fascinating instance of the relationship of structure to agency is that people perceive structures as apart from themselves, not as a product of their agency, especially when they do not participate directly in their change. For example, Germans in the East and West learned about the opening of the Wall while watching television. On the other hand, when people participate actively, they can literally see, hear, and feel structural changes: for example, after long revolutionary battles and the collapse of sovereigns. Changes in objective structures are often suddenly caused by political changes that have a huge impact on personal lives. In sudden changes, the lack of actualization of habitus is clearer than in slow, long-lasting processes of change.

Three interviewees in Austria described changes in objective structures that were decisive facilitators of their educational upward mobility. In one interviewee's life, two structural changes had great impact on his educational upward mobility.

Table 4.4 Interviewees whose educational upward mobility was largely facilitated by change in objective structures

Georg Amlang (male)	born 1928	in Austria	Mother: no information on education; day laborer (ESeC 9)
			Father: skilled carpenter; ill and unemployed (ISCED 453; ESeC 10)
Hans Pellar (male)	born 1941	in Austria	Mother: probably compulsory school; farmer (ESeC 5)
			Father: probably compulsory school; farmer (ESeC 5)
Christine Gruber (female)	born 1954	in Austria	Mother: probably compulsory school; housewife (ESeC 10)
			Father: skilled accounting clerk (ISCED 453; ESeC 7)

The first life history illustrates a comparatively sudden change as well as a slower change, the latter being true also for the second life history, while the third focuses on the change of the education system in Austria. As in all the other life histories, educational upward mobility cannot be reduced to one factor but must be seen as a complex process of interrelated circumstances. I concentrate on the most enabling dimension only to illustrate it in detail.

4.2.1 National Socialism allowed some to escape poverty

Georg Amlang is the eldest interviewee, born in 1928 in the district of a small town in upper Austria. His mother was a day laborer on several farms, and his father a skilled carpenter. Both probably completed compulsory school, but Amlang did not mention it during the interview. His brother was seven years older than he and his sister four years younger. His father was ill and unemployed; he belonged to the large group of *Ausgesteuerte*, people who did not qualify for any social welfare benefits. In 1937, half of all the unemployed belonged to this group (Tálos, 2000, p. 378). The family lived off his mother's income, and the family were allowed to use 150 steps in a potato field if they worked a day and a half for the farmer; 100 steps required one day's work. Up to his tenth birthday, Amlang wore nothing but hand-me-downs.

I got clothes from – and, that is, he still is alive; he was the son of a bricklayer, who always worked, and from him we got clothes, clothes, yes, but I actually – We had food; I got something to eat during the *Hauptschule* break; we had a cow, a pig, and chicken, and in summers I gleaned, you know what that is? When the farmers harvested, wheat, for example, they stacked the sheaves, and there were in fact very few stacks left in the field, and these we all, all, we went and gathered them and threshed them in the mill. Once I managed to get 30 kilos in a summer. We naturally went barefoot; we didn't mind in the summer, yes, and so we just, one thing is clear, there was no coffee and during the week, the famous sour soup, that's flour and cream, stirred. There was coffee only on Sundays; meat only on one Sunday.

Organized by the *Vaterländische Front*, a group following on from the *Christlichsoziale Partei*, which was banned in 1933, his family visited other families and received a meal on Sundays.

In 1938, when Austria became part of the German Reich, Amlang's father got a job. This change in political and economic structures improved Amlang's life tremendously: 'and there was also aid to children; we immediately had electricity; we immediately had, ah, a shoemaker immediately came to us, and then I got my first pair of new shoes, so the year 1938 was very decisive, because my father immediately got a job'. The family replaced the roof of the house, getting rid of the thatch.

What happened to Amlang was not individual luck but part of a political and economic change that occurred with Nazi dictatorship in Austria. When Hitler came to Linz, the nearest large city in upper Austria on 12 March 1938, tens of thousands greeted him. According to Kepplinger (2000, p. 219), Hitler's arrival was embedded in various immediate publicity measures. For example, 1.2 million Schillings were approved for the *Nationalsozialistische Volkswohlfahrt*, a Nazi welfare organization, and dispensed as cash, food, and clothing for the *Ausgesteuerte*. In the 10 April 1938 referendum, 99.6 per cent of voters were in favor of the so-called *Anschluss* (Haas, 2000). Amlang remembered that day: 'I can also remember the political situation: the referendum of 10th April 1938. My mother said, "I have always voted *Vaterländisch*, but now I'm voting yes", and my father said, "I have always voted for the Socialists, but now I'm voting yes"'. A year later, when Amlang was 11, he went to a children's camp in Bavaria for six weeks. It was the first time in his life he left his small town and lived without existential worries. Upper Austria began to industrialize (Kepplinger, 2000). According to Tálos (2000), the national unemployment rate was up to 22 per cent in 1937, and 11 per cent were *Ausgesteuerte*, who from 1938 on received state welfare benefits like child and marriage support. Moser (1995) reports that employment-creation measures aimed to integrate Austria's economy with the German armament and military industries. In upper Austria, the unemployment rate was 18.2 per cent in December 1937 and 5 per cent by the end of 1938. The municipal employment-creation program was funded at 4.5 million Reichsmark and, in the area of public and private building renovation, unemployment declined most: 'from end of June to end of September 1938 by more than 91%' (Moser, 1995, p. 61, my translation). As a carpenter, Amlang's father clearly benefited from this policy.

In Amlang's milieu, rural poverty, pupils typically went to one comprehensive school, called a *Volksschule* (ISCED 1 to 243), for their entire compulsory education. A baker's companion who knew Amlang from the Nazi youth organization asked Amlang's mother whenever he met her to send her son to the *Hauptschule*, a lower secondary school, but a stage higher than the *Volksschule*. Finally, Amlang's mother agreed, and Amlang went to a school beyond his origins and social milieu for two years. He was qualified to receive all school materials without paying. I asked whether not paying was stigmatized.

GA: No, you went downstairs; for example, when I had filled a notebook, I went to the office and received a notebook.

AK: Wasn't that demeaning?

GA: No, no, no, no, we had a very enthusiastic headmaster. Under the Nazis, there was an hour of the nation on Mondays...

What was new with National Socialism was the possibility of gaining an apprenticeship and becoming a skilled worker instead of remaining a farmhand or a maid, as his elder siblings did. He became a skilled carpenter. Having a profession, being respectable, earning a comparably high salary, participating in the new liturgy and rites of the Catholic Youth, all widened his perspective and enabled him to start evening school, where he earned the highest school-leaving degree, enabling him to study at a university and later launch a professional career.

4.2.2   Modernization of the Catholic Church as a dimension of upward social mobility

The second objective structural change that was decisive for Amlang's educational upward mobility took place after the war, at the start of the Second Republic of Austria. In 1947, Amlang was 19 and worked as a skilled carpenter in a market town close to the town where he grew up. There, he got in touch with, and engaged in, the *Katholische Jugend*, a branch of *Katholische Aktion*, a reform movement of the Catholic Church. His parents, mainly his mother, were very religious Catholics, and during his schooldays he was one of four out of 30 pupils who attended religious classes, which was exceptional in the National Socialist period.

Katholische Aktion was created to replace clubs or associations that were forbidden by the Nazis but not rebuilt after 1945 because, with the priest as secretary, they were often thinly veiled arms of the *Christlichsoziale Partei*. According to Zinnhobler (2005), Ferdinand Klostermann, who had lived in Berlin during the Third Reich, was called by the bishop of Linz to be deputy leader of pastoral care. He worked with great enthusiasm and designed the new *Katholische Aktion*. His objectives, to overcome exhaustion and resignation, soon became official. The *Katholische Jugend* departed from traditional Catholicism with new ideas and new rites, mainly involving the participation of laypersons.

On 29 May 1949 on Hauptplatz in Linz, an event with the motto '*Reine Jugend— Starkes Volk*' [Pure Youth–Strong Nation] drew 25,000 young people to celebrate the Eucharist. In the afternoon, a service in the New Cathedral was packed. Amlang described it:

> The atmosphere of a new awakening was both in the liturgy – at that time, these new masses emerged – praying and singing mass, this was unknown before, so my mother used to sit inside and read the prayer book and leave. And now suddenly these praying and singing masses emerged – we even stood in the corridor and prayed there – this was an enormous provocation to our parents, unbelievable – so this awakening in the *Katholische Jugend*, that you had a different way of celebrating Mass, that you – yes, we got around also, I can remember the State Youth Day in Linz, where

there were 30,000 people, yes, we toured everywhere and from there we founded the *Katholische Jugend*. We founded the Union, the sports club, and so on – so everything – tremendous atmosphere of awakening among an incredible number of people, at a parish party there were six, seven hundred people, that's unimaginable today. Unimaginable!

The pastoral letter about *Katholische Aktion* was read in all congregation services on 15 October 1950. On 22 October 1950, the first diocese application took place. Its motto was *'An die Arbeit! Baut in allen Pfarren unserer Diözese ... die Katholische Aktion auf. Eure Bischöfe rufen euch'* [Go to work! Build the Catholic Action in all congregations of our diocese ... Your bishops call you] (cited in Zinnhobler, 2005, p. 138).

Sunday services were generally held in Latin, but on weekdays half-German services were held. Here, a prayer leader read the Latin liturgical texts in German.

That was – but I remember how my mother talked with another, saying, 'So, what they do today, this is impossible. They stand up in the corridor', and, yes, and then we naturally bought a Schott, the special missal, that in former times, only the rich had a Schott, right? We bought a Schott, and there were new missals, prayer books, Path of Life, and so on. We prepared on a Saturday for Mass on Sunday – no, this was an incredible departure within the *Katholische Jugend*.

Many people described being able to understand the texts spoken in Mass and to participate instead of passively listening to Latin words as a liberating and uplifting experience. The new Mass elements were reconfirmed with the first document of the Second Vatican Council in 1964.

A second important dimension of the *Katholische Jugend* was the fact that sermons expressed new ideas. Harnoncourt, who studied theology from 1949 to 1954 in Graz and later became professor of liturgical science there, describes this period:

Right after the war, interest in church life suddenly woke up. It was not difficult at all to take classmates to interesting sermons at the cathedral in the evenings: Otto Mauer, the Dominican P., Diego Hans

Goetz, the Capuchin P., Heinrich Suso Braun, Georg Hansemann, Leo Pietsch auxiliary bishop in Graz in 1948, to name just a few, were listened to with such great pleasure and attention that often one had to arrive at the cathedral ten minutes early just to find a place to stand. And we often discussed these sermons for days. But when I wanted to take friends or classmates to Mass on Sunday mornings, the response was almost zero. (1996, p.198, my translation)

Amlang mentions Otto Maurer, Diego Goetz, and Suso Braun as exciting people.

Third, in addition to liberation and intellectual stimulation, the *Katholische Jugend* meant social capital to Amlang. There, he became very close to someone who went to upper secondary school in the evening; they founded the sports club Union together. Amlang was very interested in what his friend learned at school – for example, natural history – and, after accidentally finding an old newspaper story describing the first class's promotion, he felt the wish to go there. He discussed it with his friend, who encouraged him to go and to obtain the highest school-leaving certificate that would open university study to him. Amlang quit his job and moved to the nearby district capital, where he managed to find a job and to enrol in the evening school. During the day, he worked, and from 17:45 to 22:00, he had classes. On weekends, he studied. After five years, he obtained his degree, secured grant support, and went to study in Vienna: 'in principle, I wanted to study history, but I calculated, I am behind by six years, no, because of evening school, six years behind. If I go into the public sector, then I will always be missing those six years, yes, so I will study law, then I can go into the private business sector, but I was also interested in law'.

The public service income scheme in Austria is highly regulated according to age and years of employment. Amlang knew he could not make up for the 'missing' years and opted to study a subject that would lead to a higher income.

In Vienna, he joined the *Katholische Hochschuljugend* (Catholic University Youth) and served as the leader for law students for two years. He got to know interesting people, who took him to the opera and the *Burgtheater*. He enjoyed these cultural events; a new world opened. One friend and his family, who introduced Amlang to a bourgeois lifestyle, were crucial for his change of habitus:

a fellow student who sat next to me said, 'You – we have had always a student in our house who had lunch with us on Sundays, but he has finished his studies. Do you want to come to us?' Right next to me – and then I was in L. the family – the friend later became district mayor in M. – there I was welcomed, and they were a culturally very interested, a bourgeois family with enormous interest in culture. The father was director of the National Archives, and the mother was a teacher, and all of them had been to university, so culturally very interested, and – also music, I came into contact in Vienna because they, I remember, took me once to Bruckner's Fourth, this was – Vienna is – sometimes when I meet someone who says he studied in Vienna and says he doesn't like it, I can't understand it because Vienna was something very special to me.

Having lunch on Sundays with another family was familiar to him from his poor childhood, when he would go with his parents and siblings. He did not feel ashamed because being poor is not stigmatized in Christian thinking, and he could enjoy the new world opening up for him. As both his parents were dead, he was less bound to his old milieu; the lack of actualization of his original habitus facilitated his change of habitus.

One person whom he got to know when he was leader of the *Katholische Hochschuljugend* in Vienna was crucial to the introduction and spread of *Katholische Aktion* in Upper Austria. This man not only shared Amlang's engagement in the organization and cultural events, but contributed crucially to his employment in a company where he made rapid progress and stayed until retirement. Klostermann provided pastoral care to the Catholic Academic Organization, whose general director asked him whether he knew someone who would be interested in starting in this company. Initially, Amlang wanted to work for the Austrian *Arbeiterkammer*, the largest national labor organization, but he was told he would not have a chance of succeeding because he was not a Social Democrat.

While National Socialism brought an end to poverty in Amlang's family, providing the foundation for participation in education, the *Katholische Jugend* developed his mind and his sense, other prerequisites for education. It also brought very concrete contact with powerful men who enabled him to leave his milieu and to move socially upward.

4.2.3   Modernization of agriculture and staggering job losses

This section illustrates how a slow change in objective structures can enable educational upward mobility. Hans Pellar was born in 1941 in a village of about 1,000 in Upper Austria. His parents had a medium-sized farm, a *Vierkanthof*, typical of the region, which was entirely dedicated to agriculture. His mother worked the farm with help of forced laborers while his father served as a soldier. Pellar had a sister, two years older than he. The area's strong Protestant tradition was quite exceptional in Catholic Austria. In the year Pellar was born, a mass rally celebrating the third anniversary of the *Anschluss* brought Goebbels to speak, and Hitler made a surprise appearance (Lehr, 2004). In Linz, the nearest large city, the first blast furnace of the *Göring Werke* was inaugurated. Although food ration cards were in high demand, Pellar, growing up on a productive farm, did not suffer from shortages. In 1947, when he was six years old, his younger brother was born. Austria has a long tradition of principal heir law; in this locale, the youngest son inherits the whole farm. Pellar grew up knowing that he would not inherit the farm as a matter of course: 'I knew – somehow one recognizes or realizes that – this was, in that area, the way that the youngest son ... is going to be the successor. I realized this somehow, that I, if I stay at home, yes, but what is going to happen to me, no, the farm is going to my brother. As such I didn't mind, but I preferred not to stay at home. But I had to stay at home and I did my work then.' Thus, his brother's birth became the foundation for Pellar's upward educational mobility.

The principal heir law was adopted during the time of National Socialism, and ethnic, sexist, and behavioral regulations were added; some of the sexist elements were abolished in 1943 because of rural depopulation. In 1958, a federal law supported the principal heir law everywhere but in Carenthia and Tyrol, taking into account local customs privileging the eldest or youngest son. Usually, siblings who could not inherit the farm stayed to work on it or left when they married. However, modernization of agriculture, started during National Socialism and continuing after the war in what was called 'the long 1950s', from 1947 to the mid-1960s, increasingly drove family members from the farm (Hanisch, 1994). Mechanization was the decisive dimension. The use of mowers increased by over 100 per cent between 1930 and 1946 (Langthaler, 2000, p. 361). Later, when Pellar was between 12 and 26 years old, the use of mowers increased by 2,565 per cent (Kröger, 2006, p. 291). During this period, the use of tractors increased by 619 per cent; barn cleaners, 5,756 per cent; and milking machines, 1,006 per cent.

Langthaler (2000) points to an important condition for the use of machines in agriculture: a new ethic. While an earlier motto was 'work to live', the new ethic, starting with National Socialism, was 'live to work'. According to Langthaler, 'Rationalisation of the farms was impossible without rationalisation of the people' (p. 361). Rationalization was enforced through two strategies: policies of debt relief that built up market orders to integrate farms into larger than regional markets, and a systematic educational offensive delivering an image of the 'rational person' meant to replace the old work ethic of effort and frugality. However, these principles contradicted policies: on the one hand, the principal heir law compartmentalized against capitalist markets; on the other, the mechanization promoted in the four-year plan of 1936 aimed to integrate farms into state-governed goods, labor, and financial markets (p. 368). Of these two opposing objectives, the latter won out due to food shortages during and after the war.

According to Butschek (1985), the modernization of agriculture continued during the 1950s. Austria benefited after the war, first from United Nations Relief and Rehabilitation Administration (UNRRA) support, mainly seeds and fertilizers, and later from the European Recovery Program (ERP), known as the Marshall Plan. Butschek asserts that the intensity of modernization was largely due to comprehensive education and counselling measures by representatives of Austrian agriculture (pp. 195–6).

In the 1960s, a basic dilemma in agricultural policy arose: how to maintain a wealthy farming community when markets could not accommodate the increased productivity (Kröger, 2006, p. 298). According to Butschek's assessment, 'the dramatic decrease of employees in farming and forestry after the second World War was not only a clear illustration of such a process of adaptation, but on the other hand a crucial precondition for the fast economic growth up to the mid-1970s' (p. 196).

Pellar grew up in the midst of decreased opportunities in agriculture, which forced him to develop an alternative course. He benefited from evening school, the same one that Amlang and Moser attended. Pellar knew he would not inherit the farm, and even the option, open to nonhereditary siblings a generation before, to work on his brother's farm was very unlikely. He was 18 years old and had finished compulsory school at 14. For four years, he worked on the farm without a proper view to his future and began to search for something new, something else. Continuing from the previous quotation: 'and didn't I actually, actually look around, but eventually I heard that there was this school and then once with my brother-in-law – my sister was already married, and my brother-in-law was a teacher – he drove to this school with me – alone I would not have had the courage, you know – and I asked, and they said this takes nine semesters, yes, that was the regular period of school, and I said, yes, I want to do this, and I started'.

Pellar sought something unfamiliar, but he had the support of a family member. During the day, he worked on the farm and, in the evening, went to school. During the fall, the work load was tremendous, despite the machines, but in winter he was able to sleep longer in the morning. He fulfilled his military service relatively late, starting at 19, because his younger brother went away to agriculture school, and he had to stay on the farm. Stationed close to the city where the evening school was, he was allowed to continue his evening studies. In 1963, his father's childless cousin offered him his farm. Pellar moved there under the condition that he be allowed to continue studying, but, after four or five months, decided he did not like it and moved back home, finishing his studies in February 1964.

He worked for a couple of months as a delivery man for a large wine company to earn the cash he always needed and did not wish to ask his parents for. In the fall term, he went to a large city to study civil engineering. Some friends from elementary school were on the course and he thought he might have a talent for it, as he felt secure in calculating, but he found the faculty very large and anonymous, and after a month he quit and moved to the smaller veterinary school. Pellar explained the change:

It was simply too impersonal. You know, I must to say, at the vets it was – we were, I believe, in one semester, who started there, we were 40 or 50 people and those who started before us, of course almost everybody – everybody knew each other very well, even whole cohorts, but because we were so few, it was completely different. And that changed relatively, even in my time, but when I started, it was so – there were, I would say, I believe, not even 300 students. I can't say now with certainty. All right? And that was actually easier for me, I must say, and it was certainly, because of course I was always in the countryside, I was not a city person and so, yes.

He said that the decision to study was somehow normal: 'so, for me it was always, there was never any question that I would go to university, right? Never thought I would be doing something else. It was taken for granted.'

Such certainty is generally a consequence of growing up in a middle-class family with educated parents. The fact that Pellar was so decisive may be due to the duration of change of objective structures during his upbringing, which forced him to develop a new perspective on his life. Here, social change did not happen suddenly; the individual perspective grew with societal change over a long period. Even the offer to inherit his father's cousin's farm did not change Pellar's long-term course against the background of the general decrease in farming. As a matter of course, his gender was crucial, too; a woman from a farm would be unlikely to study, as confirmed when he described his sister's good performance and marks in school and her unfulfilled wish to learn. Additionally, in 1963, a year before he started his studies, state grants were introduced to support farm children. He benefited some time later, but considered it unjust because his parents earned enough to pay for his education. In contrast to Amlang, he remained close to his roots. After veterinary school, he moved near to his former village to work on a poultry farm, an area supported by the government since a 1961 agriculture law focused on abating animal diseases (Kröger, 2006, p. 293).

4.2.4 Working-class-friendly educational policies

A change of objective structures, an institutional change initiated by educational policy, enabled the educational upward mobility of Christine Gruber. She was born in 1954 in a small village close to a market town in Upper Austria, part of the Soviet Occupation Zone until 1955, when Austria became an independent state. Her mother, a housewife, was the youngest of five children born to wealthy farmers. Her father was the third of ten children born to poor farmers. During the war, he was educated in agriculture and, later, accounting, which was his highest degree. He worked in a cement factory as a manager. Gruber had to take care of her three siblings.

From December 1945 to 1966, Austria was governed by a coalition of the two main parties, the more conservative *Österreichische Volkspartei* (ÖVP) and the *Sozialistische Partei Österreichs* (SPÖ), which, in 1991, changed its name to the *Sozialdemokratische Partei Österreichs*. From 1966 to 1970, the ÖVP governed alone; from 1970 to 1983, the SPÖ governed during what was called the Kreisky era. From 1983 to 1987, the SPÖ formed a coalition with the right-wing *Freiheitliche Partei Österreichs* (FPÖ), then commenced a 13-year grand coalition government with the ÖVP under the leadership of the SPÖ until 2000, when shorter and longer coalitions, some between the ÖVP and FPÖ, devolved in 2007 to a SPÖ–ÖVP coalition again led by the SPÖ. Coalition governance is a crucial feature of Austrian society, and the practice of coming to agreements rather than holding to clear differences has a strong impact on society.

The educational policy that enabled Gruber's upward mobility was the *Schulorganisations-gesetz* [school organization law] enacted in 1962 under an ÖVP minister of education but resulting from discussions between the two large parties that began in 1946–7 (Loew, 2013). In 1948, both parties presented drafts that agreed on several points, such as abolition of school and university fees, but diverged on others, such as the organization of secondary schools. Prior to enactment of the law, a treaty between the Republic of Austria and the Holy See assured the church the right to teach the Catholic religion in public schools (Loew, 2013). Catholic education was funded by the state.

Another agreement that preceded the signing of the school organization law was a constitutional decision stipulating that school laws must be approved by at least half of the members of the parliament by a two-thirds majority. Since Austria is mainly ruled by coalition governments, no single party can impose a school policy that is not widely agreed to. This consent orientation is another strong feature of Austrian culture.

By and large, the 1962 school organization law was linked to the education law of the First Republic (1918–34) and legalized the existing school system (Scheipl & Seel, 2004, p. 26). It also introduced some reforms that affected Gruber's life history, embedded in Austrian society from the mid-1950s to the mid-1970s, when she earned her university degree. Article 4 of the school organization law stipulates that girls may be educated at any school. During the First Republic, girls were explicitly allowed to go to boys' schools, but from 1934 to 1945 the National Socialists supported gender separation as well as discrimination and exclusion of girls and women in education. Article 4 was the precondition for Gruber's education.

From 1960 to 1964, she went to the *Volksschule* (elementary school) in her town. In 1964, there were still 2,000 elementary schools in which all four or even eight grades were taught by a single teacher in a single classroom; only in Vienna were all pupils aged six to nine educated in an elementary school with four grades. Everywhere else, more than half of all children in the federal states went to elementary schools in which more than one grade was taught in one classroom (Kozlik, 1965, pp. 17–18). In Upper Austria, out of every 100 pupils, 44 went to elementary schools of four grades and nine to elementary schools of eight grades in the 1962–3 school year (p. 318). Gruber is one of the latter; her *Volksschule* comprised eight years. A year later, 72 per cent of all pupils went to elementary schools, 21 per cent to *Hauptschule* (lower secondary school, ISCED 244 for the upper stream), 2 per cent to a special needs school, and 5 per cent to an upper secondary school (ISCED 344) (*Österreichisches Statistisches Zentralamt*, 1965, p. 376).

Although 35 per cent of all children lived where the *Volksschule* was the only school, Gruber grew up in a town that had a lower secondary school as well. Her father's mother was also very interested in education and reading, and, when Gruber was about nine years old, her paternal grandparents inherited a house with an attic full of books, which she read secretly.

Article 5 of the school organization law stipulated that education in public institutions was free. Gruber's father's low income had to maintain a family of six, but, later, it improved; when Gruber was 17, her father owned and ran a small kiosk. After four years of elementary school (1960–4), she moved onto lower secondary school (*Hauptschule*). She had poor eyesight, which made reading difficult, but her teacher gave her the good mark necessary for moving up to *Hauptschule*. This step was crucial for her educational upward mobility. The *Hauptschule* was streamed; article 15 stipulated that performance in the main subjects of German, mathematics, and one foreign language should be differentiated in at least two but, better, three groups. Article 16 prescribed that the highest-performance group should be taught the same curriculum as in the upper (in the sense of both performance and age) secondary schools. It enabled the upper-stream pupils to continue studying at the upper secondary schools in grade nine; the lower secondary schools ended with grade eight.

This article, prolonging compulsory school from eight years to nine, was tremendously important. Since 1869, compulsory school had been limited to eight years, but, of every 100 pupils educated at the *Volksschule*, 72 did not proceed after the sixth grade, and only two achieved the eighth grade (Kozlik, 1965, p. 23). A new institution was created, the polytechnical school, which provided ninth-grade education mainly in preparation for vocational education. Pupils who went to the so-called Poly were generally not moving up but simply receiving an extra year of general and vocational preparation. The new requirement of a ninth year increased the possibility of attending upper secondary school rather than the Poly.

Here, finally, the amendment of the school organization law most crucial for Gruber and many others kicks in: the creation of another institution, the *Oberstufenrealgymnasium* (ISCED 344). Its musical pedagogy aimed to prepare students for the *Pädagogische Akademien*, institutions for the education of future elementary school teachers, or for later education in social professions. It also awarded the highest general school-leaving certificate, providing access to all universities, and not restricted to teacher or social worker training. The new educational institution aimed to increase the number of students in upper secondary and tertiary education (Seel & Scheipl, 1988, p. 69). The motto was 'each district shall have its own upper secondary school'. In many districts without the eight-year form of upper secondary education, the *Gymnasium*, many music-pedagogical, four-year *Oberstufenrealgymnasiums* were founded. In 1967, one year before Gruber finished *Hauptschule*, such an upper secondary institution was founded in her market town. It opened her way to higher education. According to Scheipl, this form of school 'became the key instrument for improving educational chances in rural areas in general and especially for girls'. In 1970–1, 598 *Oberstufenrealgymnasien* classes educated 18,617 pupils, of whom 11,175 were girls; of the 38,840 pupils at traditional *Gymnasien*, 14,818 were girls. In 1970, 3,577 pupils earned the highest school-leaving certificate at such institutions, 2,255 of them girls. Traditional *Gymnasien* had the share of 438% of women. (Prenner et al. 2000). As Gruber said, 'Yes, it was stroke of luck that a year before I reached *Gymnasium*, one was founded in P. And yes, our neighbor was my teacher at *Hauptschule* and the friend of my father, and he motivated my father to support this.' This quote illustrates that, apart from material conditions and the new educational institution, the teacher talking with parents and, in Gruber's case, her father's approval were decisive.

Of her class at the *Oberstufenrealgymnasium*, Gruber said: 'At *Gymnasium* there was a group – it was not constant, but they formed a clique, they organized things, not as exclusive as before, but if we did not participate, we would not have been invited to their parties, or yes, there was one –, there was one of them came in a car, no one else – and from that clique, most went to university and from the other group, most became teachers. There was a huge lack of teachers, and yes.'

The end of this quote indicates the dimension of backwardness and lack of teachers criticized by the OECD study 'Educational planning in Austria— Pedagogical planning and economic growth in Austria 1965–1975' as the cause of the unsatisfactory quantitative enhancement of upper secondary schools in Austria (Seel & Scheipl, 2004, p. 27). Teaching was a typical working-class profession, as it was familiar – as Melanie Nind pointed out to me, everyone has had teachers and experienced school – and future employment seemed secure because of the shortage.

In 1972, Gruber earned her highest school-leaving certificate. The year before, her father had opened the kiosk, and the family's economic situation had improved. Despite her father's wishes, she did not want to become a teacher; she wanted to study in a city far from home and would even have studied education in those circumstances, but she was so sure her parents would not allow it that she did not want to ask them about it. She moved to the closest city university, about 35 kilometers away, and first stayed in an aunt's flat, then moved to a student dorm. She began studying business administration and mathematics but soon quit because, as a woman, she saw no chance for a career, and she lacked confidence. Instead, she studied *Wirtschaftspädagogik*, a combination of economics, business, and pedagogy that would lead to a position as a vocational schoolteacher.

She graduated in 1977 and began working at a school in another town. She would have liked to work in adult education, but was too young. For a while, she commuted to the city to study philosophy, but dropped out. She was also interested in becoming a psychologist and took some classes in this area, but, since she had started a family, she did not achieve a degree. At the time of the interview, she was a vocational school teacher and ambivalent about her work:

> Well [5-second pause], well, what form does it take? [10-second pause] Yes, I find it often difficult to give bad marks, to fail students. This – with this or with marking in general, I somehow thought my task is to give children opportunities and not to select and exclude them. I have problems, even today somehow, no. Then, in my appearance, my outfit, I don't like, I still don't, somehow, yes, being dressed up – I don't feel very comfortable. In language, yes, even in school, I drop into dialect pretty quickly. Of course, I know that students understand me better then, and when something is difficult, I quickly switch to dialect. In the early years, generally not, but only – from university – only speaking proper German, but I changed relatively quickly. This is always a somewhat elitist sign, so this elitist stuff, I have not really integrated – I don't like it.

Her words remind us of the difficulties of social upward mobility, ambivalent and full of compromises with the original milieu. She did not study the subject or attend the university she would have chosen. She was painfully conscious of reproducing social inequality through education and her own involvement as an educationally upwardly mobile woman.

Here, the emergence of the new and social change are clearly linked to educational reforms, such as the extension of compulsory school years and the expansion of upper secondary schools in rural areas, with musical and artistic concentrations that especially attracted girls. Gruber benefited from these reforms. The new was seeded in her father's family: he was a skilled employee, the only one among his siblings, and her paternal grandmother, who was intellectually curious and well-read, valued and encouraged her granddaughter. However, Gruber was not free to study or to move away. On the maternal side, she experienced no encouragement and a lot of distrust and devaluation. Altogether, the new was highly ambivalent, dangerous, conflicted, and disputed. Fortunately, she was supported by two teachers who discerned her high performance and gave her good marks. She did not give up and was able to compromise. However, she was not able to go far beyond her father's approval, and paid the price in not following the life course of interest. In her case, social change was limited.

4.3   Lack of actualization of habitus as a catalyst for educational upward mobility

This section illustrates a change of habitus initiated by a lack of actualization of the old habitus. It was a very slow, incremental process and a good illustration of the limits of change of habitus alluded to by Bourdieu.

Alice Clayton was born in 1957 in a large industrial city in the Midlands. After leaving school at the end of compulsory education, her mother was a pastry cook, a cleaner, and a hospital porter, and her father got a job with the British Army, working on building sites. Clayton had a sister and a brother, five and nine years younger, respectively. She took care of them and prepared them for school, since her mother started her paid work at 7:30. Her father worked full-time and went to the pub in the evening. Once a year, her mother took the kids for a week at the seaside in a caravan. Her father did not go. 'My dad never did anything with us at all', Clayton said. 'He just used to go to work, come home, and then he liked to go out and drink. So my dad didn't do anything with us at all. He didn't come on holiday with us.' He still decided that she must be in by 21.00. At home, the family did not chat or discuss daily matters. If the children wanted anything, they asked their mother to talk with their father.

Clayton failed the 11+ exam and went to a secondary school. Of the three sets, Clayton participated in the middle one, where sciences and foreign languages were not taught. She earned the Certificate in

Secondary Education (ISCED 243), below the General Certificate in Secondary Education (ISCED 244). From the outset, she did not like school; she felt overtaxed and without teacher support: 'For maths, I found that a hard subject, and if you went to the teacher and said, "Could you show me how to do it?" he'd turn round and say to you, "Oh, go and work it out yourself and go and sit down and work it out." So you never got to learn anything. I struggled with that.'

At the age of 14, she started to deliver the evening paper after school and on Sunday mornings to have some spending money. When she was 15 or 16, she joined the Navy Cadets and enjoyed it. I asked what she did apart from school:

AC: To start with, we just used to go out and walk round outdoors. Just walking round the streets, nothing to do. Then I joined the Cadets, and they used to have Army, Navy, and Air Force Cadets, and I joined the Navy Cadets from about 15, 16, and I really enjoyed that. I had a uniform, and you'd go once a week to the Navy Cadets, and it was good. From that, that made me want to join the Forces.

AK: And what did you do there?

AC: From what I can remember, obviously you had to look after your uniform, polish your shoes, and it was just learning about different things to do with the Navy and things like that and teamwork. It was good.

After compulsory school, she easily found an office job at a milk supplier and, later, with a supermarket company founded by an American who was in the Navy. A year later, at 18, she joined the Air Force and worked as a parachute packer. At 20, she married a man she met there, also employed by the British Army, and, at 22, bore their first daughter and, later, another. She quit work, and the family moved around Britain and Germany. In 1990, they divorced, marking a caesura in her life that led her to higher education. I want to focus on this caesura to illustrate how the lack of actualization of her former habitus enabled her to become educationally upwardly mobile.

The separation and divorce were socially and psychologically disruptive. Her material living conditions, as well as her social recognition and self-perception, changed. She had no income and no house. From a materially secure and respected wife, she became a single mother, without profession, job, or place to live. She also lost the Army, a social organization that made her feel important. She lost her confidence. Of the wish to improve herself and have nice things, she said:

> *AC:* I think it perhaps came after my divorce. I think perhaps my confidence went, so I wanted to get back to being somebody and improving myself and doing something and making something of myself.
>
> *AK:* So the date was really after your separation.
>
> *AC:* Yes, because I was in the Air Force so I felt important, and I had my own career and even being married and having children and still travelling around with my husband with the Air Force, I still felt fine. But when we separated and I came back to S., I had nowhere to live. I had to stay with my family for a couple of weeks, but you used to have a waiting list to go in a Council house and because I had my name on a waiting list for 12 years when we first got married, that enabled me to get a Council house. But it wasn't a very nice house, and I'd been used to living in nice accommodation with the Air Force, going to places with my husband, wearing ball gowns, and then suddenly I had nothing again. Nothing. So I'd gone from having a poor background as a child to going into the Air Force, earning money, getting married, having nice things, and then divorced, I was back to nothing again. Living in a horrible house, no money. And I had to start again and work myself up. So I think that's why I always want to do better. I could accept that and accept that that's my way of life, I've got nothing, I don't want to. I want to have nice things, and I think if you're determined, you can improve your life. But you have to work hard though to do that.

In 1977, when Clayton married, the large majority of British women over 16 were married. The usual female pattern of life was to have children within the married couple. At the same time, 55 per cent of all married women between 18 and 24 years old were economically active. Of all married women aged 16–34 with dependent children, 9 per cent worked full-time and 29 per cent part-time (Office of Population Censuses and Surveys, 1979). The gender wage gap was tremendous; in April 1977, full-time weekly earnings in all industries and services were £76.80 for men and £50.00 for women (Department of Employment, 1977). Marriage, having children, and becoming a housewife was the normal way of life. Clayton's marriage enabled her to move up socially; unlike her mother, she did not have to work outside the house; she travelled and enjoyed social events and middle-class material conditions such as nice clothes. Objective structures, such as gender relations, division of labor by gender, and state support of heterosexual marriage, rewarded a confirmatory lifestyle. Although these structures were being questioned by the feminist movement, Clayton's narration gives no hint that she was aware of critical and alternative views. Her upbringing, youthful career, and early marriage point to a rather traditional lifestyle in terms of gender relations. After the break up, education became a way to regain material security, respectable social status, and self-confidence. The new perspective required a change of habitus in terms of a new life perspective under now unfavorable but persistent objective structures. Like anyone, Clayton could only develop the new life perspective with the resources she had, so it developed slowly and in tandem with her old habitus. Her educational upward mobility was a slow, step-by-step process of accumulation.

> Got divorced, and I settled back in S., and then I decided to retrain, get some more qualifications, so that's when I did a typing course for six months. Then I did a leisure and recreation course Parts 1 and 2. I did a communication skills course, and that was City and Guilds those three. Then I got a job working in the leisure center in S, different ones. I started part-time because I had my two children, and I did a lot of weekend work, so my mum and dad were very good and used to look after the children for me at the weekends when I had to work. So they were very good. Sometimes, when I was working part-time, I would work just a few hours perhaps in the morning when the children were at school, so I was home for the evening. Then I got a full-time job, and the children were getting older. Still in the leisure centers. So you'd do a week of morning shifts, a week of evening shifts, and my sister was very good. She used to take my youngest to school for me or collect her from school as well, so I had help from family that way. And then when I was working at the leisure center I still wanted to carry on gaining qualifications, so they paid for a

course for me in supervising to do with the sports industry, and I used to travel to Workshop College. That was day release. I also did a sports therapy course, while I was working at the leisure centers, did all little qualifications like leadership qualifications for teaching athletics, swimming teaching course, aqua aerobics, circuit training, all things like that. Then I went to university.

Clayton did not have to pass an access course to university because of all her qualifications and the good marks she received in a supervisor's course. The fact that her employer provided day release not only made study materially possible, but also improved her confidence. A recursive, self-energizing process took place, a change of habitus in which acknowledgment in terms of material support and symbolic reward triggered her educational upward mobility. At the same time, this process was very working-class: embedded in her milieu, led by concrete objectives, such as a relevant study subject and improving income. In contrast to Amlang, Clayton's educational upward mobility was closely related to her family: her parents and her sister took care of her daughters to give her time both to work and to study. Clayton needed strong family ties to proceed as she provided sole care for two children, which also tied her locally.

From 2004 to 2007, 14 years after her divorce, she started to study Outdoor Recreation at the university in S. and earned a BSc. She funded her studies with a student loan and enjoyed them. Even though all her fellow students were much younger men, she had good relations with them and felt supported by the lecturers. She graduated with good marks.

However, afterward, she could not find an adequate job and had to work in an office to pay her debts. At the time of the interview, she was enrolled in a one-year Postgraduate Certificate in Education program, offering a degree to teach 14–19-year-olds. She paid for her study with a bursary from the university of £600 per month plus a student loan and a loan for fees. She was going to finish in summer 2010 at the age of 53.

Social change in Clayton's life history is very restricted. After her divorce, she saw education as a way to improve her low social status in two ways: improving her chances of better-paying jobs and proving to herself and others that she was able, important – she sought recognition. Her social ascent was a long, hard-fought process of small steps that did not lead her very far up in the hierarchy. Her life history shows how a lack of actualization of habitus can take place within unchanging objective structures, a possibility Bourdieu has not considered.

4.4 Becoming conscious as a motor to habitus change

As outlined in the second chapter, Bourdieu mentioned this condition as an inducement to alter habitus. As in all the other life histories of educational upward mobility, becoming conscious was not the only reason, but one of many. Nevertheless, becoming conscious of objective social structures was crucial for Beth Rogers to attend and graduate from university. The following description focuses on the social context and conditions that made her conscious.

Rogers was born in 1968 at a seaside resort in north-east England. In the interview, she described the town:

> It's quite a deprived area, and there aren't really any opportunities there. Don't get me wrong. I have fond memories, and it's by the sea, but there are no theatres. You couldn't go and see bands. There is nothing like a city has to offer. It's a very small town with not very much to offer really, and the nearest big place is either [...] or [...], and they're both 60 miles away, and there's nowhere else you can access any of the facilities that you get living in a city. So it felt like it was quite a run-down area with not many opportunities.

After completing compulsory school, her mother worked as a part-time shop assistant, but during Rogers' upbringing, she was at home, working as a housewife. She enjoyed reading and read a lot to her daughter, who loved it and developed the habit. Rogers's father was a plumber. She summarized the values of her milieu: 'I think when you grow up sometimes, especially in a small town, the values that are there are that the most important thing is to find a man, the right man, get married and have children. That's the values really that I was brought up with.' Her sister was almost 12 years older.

Rogers went to three different primary schools because her parents kept moving from one house to another. She found this experience quite disturbing, partly because she lost touch with friends and partly because her classes proceeded at different speeds. She was bored at her third school because the content was completely familiar. From 1980 to 1985, she went to the nearest secondary school. Her parents could no longer help her with her homework, but they paid for extra lessons:

> Once I got to secondary school, I think the work I was doing was just beyond my parents really. They didn't understand it. But what they did do – I know I was struggling at maths at one point, and they actually got me some extra lessons. I remember coming home upset about not being able to do the maths, and they got me some extra lessons. They couldn't understand it themselves because they hadn't done it, so they couldn't help in that way, but they were very supportive of that, and I always got a sense that they were very proud of me, and when they went to parents' evening and things, they were pleased that I was doing well.

In 1985, when her compulsory school period ended, the labor market could not absorb any more people with only O-level qualifications (ISCED 343). This situation was a crucial reason for continuing formal education or getting a job. In Austria, masses of young people can receive systematic, well-regarded, and, in certain areas, well-remunerated vocational education. In contrast, England has a small, undeveloped vocational education sector, which means that the alternative after compulsory education is mainly work. For the unemployed, the government ran special vocational programs. During the mid-1980s, education policy was dominated by the Conservative government of Margaret Thatcher (1979–90). Gillard (2011) characterizes its education policy as 'marketization'. Referencing Benn and Chittey, from 1977 to 1989, a huge amount of money was spent on the Technical and Vocational Education Initiative: 25 schemes were introduced and 22 abolished, sometimes very quickly. In 1986, the National Council for Vocational Qualifications promoted National Vocational Qualifications to be obtained at work and General National Vocational Qualifications to be provided at schools, but no integration of academic and vocational education took place.

Today, general qualifications are more highly valued and carry greater prestige than vocational qualifications. At the end of the

1970s and again in the 1980s, to deal with the masses of young people who dropped out but could not find a job, the government created the Youth Opportunities Programme (YOP) and, later, the Youth Training Scheme (YTS). In 1984–5, only 16 per cent of 16-year-olds had a job, compared with 53 per cent in 1975–6 (Central Statistical Office, 1987, p. 61); 27 per cent participated in YTS, compared with 6 per cent in 1978–9 who had participated in the former YOP; 31 per cent were school and 14 per cent in nonadvanced further education (p. 60). More girls than boys were enrolled in formal education.

From 1985 to 1987, Rogers went to a sixth form college in her small town. She took A levels in English, history, and politics. English was her favorite subject, and she remembers the texts they read and discussed in class. At the same time, her sister's husband left his wife and their two small children. Rogers was very angry at her former brother-in-law for years. She became aware of the objective structures that affected her sister's miserable living situation: the lack of free or affordable public childcare, the lack of jobs that would allow her sister to earn an income sufficient to run a family of three, and the poor odds of obtaining such a job without a higher educational degree.

> Seeing what happened to my sister was kind of, 'Well, it's not all rosy and happy. Things can go bad', and I wanted to be able to not be reliant on a man and be independent myself. I had this kind of feeling that I wanted to be able to earn my own money and set myself up and be independent and not be in the situation that she was now in because she was in a situation where she wasn't working because she had two small children, but she didn't have any qualifications to fall back on, and her whole life had been mapped out with being married and having children. When that fell apart, there was nothing there for her. I think it just made me feel that I didn't want to be in that position and wanted to make sure that I could do something for myself.

In 1985, out of every 1,000 married people in the UK, 13.4 were divorced (Central Statistical Office, 1987, p. 49). In 1971, when Rogers' sister was 15 years old, a year before leaving school, the divorce rate had been less than half that, at 6 per 1,000 married people in England and Wales (Halsey, 1987, p. 13). By the time she had decided to go the 'marriage path', it looked much more secure; divorces were the exception, and most petitions were filed by wives, not husbands (Central Statistical Office, 1986, p. 38). Evidence shows that '[w] omen who marry younger, particularly as teenagers, tend to come from the least advantaged family backgrounds and educational and occupational careers. Thus, if their marriage dissolves, they would tend to be in poor economic circumstances' (Ermisch, 1989, p. 51). According to the Family Expenditure Survey, 'in 1984, the average income of households with children headed by one parent (90 per cent of whom are mothers) was about 40 per cent of the income of two-parent households with children (and no other person)' (Ermisch, 1989, p. 42). The Matrimonial and Family Proceedings Act in 1984 made divorce easier and quicker (Pilcher, 1999, p. 84). Lewis assesses the effect: 'The 1984 divorce legislation promoted the self-sufficiency principle and required the court to consider the earning capacity of the husband and of the wife. But while it may be attractive to attempt to "wipe the slate clean", given the gendered division of work, self-sufficiency – meaning dependence on wages – is not likely to be achievable by the vast majority of women with children' (1992, p. 103).

The amendment of divorce law took place against the backdrop of marketization in education, the retreat of the state, and cuts in social welfare. Private shoulders had to take more responsibility for young and old people; these shoulders were presumed to number four: 'On the whole, the drift of policy during the 1980s has appeared to be toward promoting the two-parent family and within this traditional roles for husbands and wives, largely by curtailing collective provision for the care of dependent family members whether young or old' (Lewis, 1992, pp. 30–1). Feminist studies on patriarchal welfare states reveal deeply embedded structures discriminating against women (Briar, 1997; Pascall, 1997; Pateman, 1992; Ungerson & Kember, 1997). In the context of these larger sociopolitical and economic structures, the divorce of Rogers' sister becomes understandable as a major incident, reducing her economic well-being and, in addition, stigmatizing her as a single mother, 'associated in both popular and psychological literature with problems of delinquency and social disorder' (Lewis, 1992, p. 33).

Rogers had a close relationship to her sister, who quit after compulsory school to work, first at a hairdresser's and later in other jobs.

Rogers admired her; she seemed glamorous and very different. Her sister married at 18 and had her first child at 19. When her husband left her, she picked Rogers up from the sixth form college and drove to the sea to tell her before telling their parents. Their closeness probably increased the impact of the incident on Rogers' life. As a consequence, she decided to seek higher education as the best way to become economically independent. Fearing that her parents would object to her leaving the small town, she applied for a place without telling them. She did not get it and finally applied to clearance, a mechanism to distribute the remaining study places to people who tend to have lower marks and cannot select a university for themselves. Through clearance, she received quite a lot of offers, but one university called her and invited her for an interview. Her father rented a car, and the whole family went on the 300-mile trip. Rogers was still insecure. She narrated her decision process:

> I remember ringing my English Lit teacher and asking him because there were offers from several other places, but because I'd been to C., it almost felt that because they'd asked me to come down for an interview and because my parents had put so much effort into coming down that I'd say yes there. So it wasn't really on any choice of whether this was a good place to go or not, it was just kind of circumstance, really.

The college was small. She studied English Literature and Religion as a combined study degree from 1987 to 1990 on a full grant. For seven months, she participated in an exchange program at a university in Kansas, US. In her third year, she went to a career adviser. She knew what she did not want to do (teaching and newspaper work) but not exactly what she wanted. She was advised to become a career adviser and participated in a year-long, postgraduate diploma course at another university, funded with the help of a loan. Upon finishing, she applied all over Britain and received a four-month post (maternity leave) with the Youth Service in a large city. At the time of the interview, she had worked there for 19 years. She managed some staff who went into schools to deliver advice and guidance and others who worked with vulnerable young people. She lived with a man who had two grown children from a previous marriage. She had no children of her own.

Clearly, the new in Rogers' life started with her consciousness of her sister's plight – left with two small children and no formal education or job. This incident had a huge impact on her perception of the world and the role of education in furthering life chances. It builds on knowledge of a world beyond her own, beyond her family and her neighborhood and village, a world she got to know through books, those her mother read to her and those she read and discussed at school. Rogers proceeded in small steps. After O levels, she went to a college as an alternative to a job, which would have been hard to find at the time. She attended the first university that called to invite her, visiting it with her whole family instead of visiting other universities as well. She did a one-year postgraduate diploma (PGDip) on a small loan rather than studying for another degree that would have taken longer and required a larger loan. She went to Kansas, rather than, say, California or staying in the city where her university was located. She took a job as a temporary replacement for someone on maternity leave, but it blossomed into a career, allowing her to stay where she was and to be promoted.

4.5   Pedagogical effort leading to educational upward mobility

Here, we address the last reason Bourdieu mentioned for a change of habitus: the efforts of teachers that influence and enable pupils to become educationally upwardly mobile. Pedagogical effort is related to individual actions and differs from what I will present later as another reason: educational institutions purposefully and politically designed to support inclusion.

Andrew Lewis was born in 1953 in a large town in North West England. His mother left school at the end of compulsory education, worked as a maid and cleaner in a pub, and became a housewife while Lewis was growing up. His father also left after compulsory school and worked as a manual laborer in a factory. Lewis was the youngest of four: sisters 20 and 14 years older than he and a brother 18 years older. The family lived in a rented flat and, when Lewis was 10, moved to a Council house. Before he was born, the family was poor – his mother frequently pawned items without his father knowing – but at the time of his birth all of his siblings were working and bringing money into the household. Lewis said he had an enjoyable childhood but described his family milieu as full of 'poverty, ignorance, bigotry'.

A self-acknowledged late developer, he started primary school at seven and remained there for five years. School opened his eyes to how poor his family was:

> when I came along things were improving. We didn't have a lot of money at all though. We were still considered quite poor. I began to notice this at school, seeing just how better clothed some of my friends were. I could really tell. Just the general quality of clothing. That's something I remember, thinking back now. They had nice cotton shirts, properly ironed, neat hair cuts, this sort of thing. So there was plenty of evidence that other people were in better circumstances. So as I grew up, through junior and into secondary school, I felt this poverty... I went through many years of feeling quite embarrassed, even ashamed sometimes, at my poor origins.

In 1965, Lewis failed the 11+ examination. A year before, in October 1965, the Labour government had taken over from the Conservatives and created a Circular (10/65) that expressed the intention to abolish the 11+ and to eliminate separation in secondary education (Chitty, 2009). At that time, most secondary institutions in England and Wales were secondary modern schools, followed by grammar schools, other secondary schools, comprehensive schools, technical schools, and some others. However, local authorities were only asked to submit *plans* for reorganizing secondary education, and no comprehensive system was ruled out compulsorily. The government also accepted plans for partial comprehensiveness, which is an oxymoron (Gillard, 2011).

Lewis entered secondary school. During the 1960s, many local education authorities decided to change from a two-tier system of primary and secondary schools to a three-tier system of first, or lower, school, middle school, and upper school. The Education Act of 1964 allowed transfer to other schools at ages other than 11 without creating a comprehensive system, and it allowed a limited experimental status to middle schools. The idea was to combine the best pupil support practices of the primary schools with better support for transitions to middle school than the 11+ allowed. Overall, the

1960s are seen as a period of 'optimism' (Gillard, 2011) and greater inclusiveness in education. In this atmosphere, Lewis experienced the first impact of 'pedagogical effort':

> There had already been one or two role models, one or two boys from my school who had made it to university. Thinking back, I remember there was one example of a boy who had been at our secondary modern school who was able by whatever means to go to the University of Leeds. I remember the headmaster telling us this great news in the hall. I can't remember his name, but in assembly – I remember this one. There may have been one or two others. So suddenly, the very idea of university was possible, but I do remember my careers teacher, who then we called youth employment officers, when I said I would quite like the idea of going on to university, so the seed was there.

The deputy headteacher from the 'posh' school, the grammar school, came to talk to the boys at the secondary school. During that time, many links between schools and college existed, some loose and others systematic. According to King (1976, p. 115), 92 per cent of colleges participated by providing information about courses and stimulating recruitment, targeting mainly secondary modern schools.

Lewis said that his youth employment officer actually did *not* support his seeking higher education but told him to think about a trade. Lewis took this advice and went alone to a further education college, where he experienced more *dis-encouragement*. His upward path was not facilitated entirely by pedagogical effort but by the opposite as well, although finally pedagogical encouragement won out. Lewis talked about his visit to a further education college:

> I remember making visits to the further education college myself to seek information and knocking on doors to try to speak to tutors who looked at me as if I'd landed from another planet. The idea of somebody taking the initiative to try and find things out, this obviously wasn't usual. But I did get a bit of information. Now it's all coming back to me. I found that response from the college tutors themselves so lacked encouragement that I felt get a decent

education there. So that's what helped me make the decision to go to the grammar school.

The assistance was rather backhanded.

During this time, the post-16 education sector expanded tremendously. According to King, the 'proportion of unskilled occupations fell from 12 per cent in 1951 to 6.6 per cent in 1971' (1976, p. 15), supporting Lipset and Zetterberg's (1966) observation that the increase in white-collar jobs changed the societal status of education. In particular, from 1965 to 1970, the number of pupils in further education colleges taking A levels rose by 86.7 per cent in the first year and by 60 per cent in second and subsequent years (Webster, 1974, p. 21). Overall, the numbers of 17-year-olds staying on in full-time secondary education rose from 10.8 per cent in 1958, to 13.5 per cent in 1964, to 20 per cent in 1970 (Schools Council Publications, 1972, p. 37). The number of students taking A levels increased by more than 60 per cent between 1962 and 1970. Although Lewis was the only family member who took A levels, he grew up during a steep national rise in A-level students. The expansion of post-16 education spread over five different types of educational institutions (pp. 26–7); by 1970, the secondary modern school was by far the most frequent choice (2,691), followed by comprehensive institutions (1,250), grammar schools (1,038), and technical colleges (82). Seven years later, the enrolment in comprehensive schools was 63 per cent, followed by 15 per cent in grammar schools (Reid & Filby, 1982, p. 158). When Lewis was studying at the secondary modern school, the secondary school population grew from 8.5 per cent in 1965 to 31 per cent in 1970 (Simon, 1991, p. 299).

From 1970 to 1972, Lewis went to a comprehensive sixth form college. From September 1970 onwards, the Council's Education Committee introduced comprehensive education for separate boys' and girls' sixth form colleges. According to the Secondary Heads Association (1979), a characteristic of comprehensive sixth form colleges is that they 'made available not only to the chosen few, but to all young people, who wish to take advantage of them, from those who relish the sixth form tradition of study in depth to those who need to develop the basic skills necessary to generate the self confidence that past mistakes may have destroyed' (81). However, Lewis's comprehensive sixth form college was not a welcoming and comfortable experience for him at the beginning.

So the two years I spent at the grammar school, the new comprehensive, it really did feel a bit like going to Oxford or Cambridge. The school had history; they had houses, groupings like a fraternity kind of arrangement, and there were six of these houses and there were the Romans, Etruscans, Parthenons, Trojans... and so we competed together in sports. Like teams, but we called them houses. It was very much based on a public school idea. We call private schools public schools in the UK, of course. So this is how the school saw itself. It was very much an ethos, part of its approach taken from the public school like Eton, Harrow, prep school. So many of the teachers were wearing gowns, their university graduation gowns, whilst teaching. In the assemblies in the morning these teachers would all be wearing their gowns. The headteacher, deputy head, wore gowns and certainly prefects would be wearing their gowns. They had special gowns, even though they hadn't yet graduated. So it was definitely trying to create this atmosphere of exclusivity, excellence, old-style, the good old grammar school idea. So for me, going into that environment, I was like 'Oh my goodness'. I felt out of my depth; it took me a while to settle, and in the first few weeks, I wanted to leave. I didn't feel at home at all.

In a case study of a former grammar school, at the time of the investigation (1974–5) a sixth form college – two years after Lewis finished his sixth form school – Francis (1976) compared the perceptions and evaluations of former grammar, secondary modern, and comprehensive school boys. He found that the former grammar school boys rated the staff–pupil relationship better than the other groups. Former secondary modern and comprehensive school boys felt that staff were less interested in listening to their ideas about college and provided fewer occasions for them to try out their new ideas compared with the former grammar school boys. The author suggested that the former grammar school boys came from within the system and were familiar with the expectations of parents and staff.

In his situation, Lewis went to the Career Office and experienced a second decisive pedagogical effort: 'but the careers' adviser there was adamant that I shouldn't leave. He talked me into staying, which was probably the right thing, I think. But I wouldn't speak to a young person that way. I would do it a different way. His advice was correct in reality, but maybe the way he didn't wasn't. So I was unhappy, but then I settled and became a lot happier.'

He described his experiences in terms of class differences: 'Yes, but in reality, the attitude of teachers was they still thought of themselves as a grammar school, behaved like grammar school teachers. The reputation of the school was fixed, going back in time, it was a very well-respected school with high achievers and a good reputation not just for learning but for sport, rugby and all that. So it was very much a class thing, a feeling there, a division of the classes.'

These class differences are the reason he felt 'not at home', 'out of his depth', and reflect the social composition of sixth form colleges at that time. A study found that in 1974, in a sample of six sixth form colleges, only 1 per cent of all students had an unskilled father (Dean et al., 1979, p. 76). Lewis did not reject the house system based on individual taste; an observational study by Davies in 1965 found 'that working class sixth formers showed lower levels of acceptance of the house system' (King, 1976, p. 42).

The careers adviser's reaction to Lewis's desire to leave must also be seen in the context of the culture and ideology of sixth form colleges at the time. According to King (1976, p. 153), the idea of community is crucial for English education in general and sixth form colleges in particular, and is linked to the integration of pastoral care. Although Lewis does not seem to have experienced this pastoral care as smoothing or soft support, but, rather, as a strict, hard attitude, it could be interpreted in the light of a community ideology as feeling responsible for all members of the college, expressed in staying adamant and talking pupils into staying. Although 76 per cent of pupils are advised by their families to stay on in full-time education, 36 per cent in the Youth Cohort Study 5 in 1989–90 followed advice from their careers offices to stay, and another 36 per cent followed advice from careers teachers (Payne et al., 1996, p. 121). These numbers are obviously taken from much later cohorts than Lewis's, but data for the study period are lacking, and these probably reflect a long-term tendency.

After finishing sixth form college, Lewis applied to university, was accepted, and studied history on a full grant from his local authority that covered fees and maintenance. In 1972–3, educational expenditure as a percentage of the Gross Domestic Product (GDP) was 5.6; in 1975–6, when Lewis finished his Bachelor's degree, it was at an all-time high in British history at 6.3 (Simon, 1991, p. 599). Clearly, Lewis benefited from a policy that prioritized education over defense (4.6 and 4.8 per cent in the respective years), for example.

He graduated with a BA Hons. in 1976; he took an additional year because he changed his subject after the first. In the following years, he lived in London because his friends moved there. He had a lot of temporary jobs and did a lot of painting and decorating, perhaps expressing his interest in art. In 1990, when he was 36, he participated in a one-year, postgraduate, full-time diploma course in Careers Guidance at a post-1992 university, which is a former polytechnic with less prestige than traditional universities. After he finished his studies, he took a job as a careers adviser in a City Council Education Office in a large city in the north of England. From there, he switched to a university and has been employed on a rolling contract since 2005.

Lewis's educational upward mobility could be seen as an ideal example of the changing political structure. In the late 1960s and early 1970s, there was a general atmosphere of reform, several profound educational reforms, and a change in teachers' and head-masters' attitudes and actions that supported educational upward mobility.

The new came into Lewis's life from two individuals: first, the deputy headmaster at the former grammar school who came to Lewis's secondary school to recruit boys; second, the career adviser who did not let Lewis leave school but talked him into staying. These new things were embedded not only in the new political structure, but also in the Lewis family's new economic circumstances, so that, by the time he was school age, they had more income because his much older siblings were contributing their pay. They had also moved to a house and left the flat, a key symbol of economic well-being and respectability in England.

The surrounding political structure brought not just concrete educational reforms but a change in attitudes and values. Lewis was exposed to a worldview very different from the one at home, which was dominated by bigotry, racism, sexism, and narrowness. He decided to live in London to be in touch with this changing mood; he listened to music that did not exist before and saw lives different from those in H. He could afford this life because of the healthy job market.

The step to becoming a career adviser is based on both new and old elements. Career advice was the crucial enabling factor for his own development, but only now does he feel confident enough to engage with the world and to become important for other people. In the past, he had just lived for the day and for himself. Old and new are crystallized in his narrative: 'I wouldn't speak to a young person that way. I would do it a different way.'

Gruber's life presents another example where pedagogical effort was crucial. We met her in Section 4.2.4 on change in educational policy as part of objective structures. One of her teachers at lower secondary school came to talk to her father to convince him to allow Gruber to go to the upper secondary school. She described this incident as crucial for her educational upward mobility:

> How this transition happened? Well, pupils with good marks were asked whether they wanted to go on to *Gymnasium*, whether they would like to enrol, as they said 'this would suit your' – somehow, they expected this of us, and yes, I know that my father talked with the neighbor, that they discussed a few things, but I never heard it directly. No relation to, but my wish was then, so this was – I want this, and there was no resistance. Although at this time some friends from *Hauptschule* did not receive permission from home, even though this teacher was after them, I know. But it was of no use.

This teacher made a difference in opening a space so that her parents' resistance diminished, and she could realize her wish to continue going to school.

4.6 Gender

In the life histories of four interviewees, gender contributed to their educational upward mobility.

We have met these three men and one woman earlier. However, I will increasingly come back to life histories, as an abundance of circumstances and conditions are crucial for upward mobility, not just one. Although for these interviewees gender was important – in

Table 4.5 Interviewees in whose lives gender was crucial for upward mobility

Georg Amlang (male)	born 1928	in Austria	Mother: no information on education; day laborer (ESeC 9)
			Father: skilled carpenter; ill and unemployed (ISCED 453; ESeC 10)
Hans Pellar (male)	born 1941	in Austria	Mother: probably compulsory school; farmer (ESeC 5)
			Father: probably compulsory school; farmer (ESeC 5)
Eric Finch (male)	born 1964	in England	Mother: compulsory school; secretary, shoe and perfume factory worker (ESeC 9)
			Father: compulsory school; mill, kitchen, and transport worker (ESeC 9)
Christine Gruber (female)	born 1954	in Austria	Mother: probably compulsory school; housewife (ESeC 10)
			Father: skilled accounting clerk (ISECD 453; ESeC 7)

Amlang's and Pellar's cases, it was requisite for accessing higher education – I assessed other circumstance and conditions as more crucial. The following description comprises three life histories in which male privileges were crucial for educational upward mobility. I proceed in the chronological order of their ages and omit Gruber's story here, as we have already examined the gender dimension of the educational policy that supported her in the section on objective changes.

4.6.1 The contribution of being male to educational upward mobility

The interviews with Amlang, born in 1928, and Pellar, born in 1941, make clear, if not explicit, that a precondition for their attendance at an evening school to acquire the highest school-leaving degree, which gave them access to higher education, was being male. This advantage is apparent when they talk about their sisters. Note that Moser's experience was different: his sister, born in 1922, went to upper secondary school and later to university, where she graduated with a PhD before migrating to Canada and Australia.

Amlang learned about the evening school by coincidence. While he and his younger sister were piling wooden pallets, an older pile of wood collapsed, and they found a copy of an old local newspaper, reporting on the graduation of the first cohort of the evening school in L. The date of this incident is not clear, but Amlang was working as a carpenter and must have been between 19 and 23 years old. He was probably closer to 23, since otherwise he might have gone to the school sooner. In any case, the timing was ideal, as he had obtained the prerequisites for study by then. In the second round of the interview, I asked whether he was with his sister when he learned about the evening school.

> With my sister. We built a new woodpile, stacking chunks of wood. We built it, and close by there was also an old pile of wood, and it collapsed, it collapsed, and I reach into it and look at this newspaper, the *Rieder Volkszeitung*, yes, and I leaf through, and at once it says – there, page – report on nature, on the first graduating class of the evening school in 1943. I read this, said, 'uh-oh'! This was unknown, the evening school, not like today, when you know about everything, it was not known.

I asked whether his sister might have felt like going to the evening school as well.

> No, it was like this: the youngest was not the best student. She struggled, of course, but she never had an interest, but I must say honestly, I never talked with her about it. She was only always against me doing it, saying, 'You want to go to Vienna, and you have no money – you are crazy.'

Later, I said I was surprised that he was the only one of the siblings who moved up educationally, and he explained:

> Yes, could have done so – actually, only my sister, the younger one, and there we actually never – she did not go to *Hauptschule* [lower secondary school], I believe, she struggled a bit, yes, but it was not so easy that she went to the *Hauptschule*, and she only

obtained *Volksschule*, yes, and our brothers are all older, and my sister, born in 1916, it was predetermined that she only would go into farming. It was impossible that she, one, generally my sister, a woman, impossible. There was no profession, no, impossible, no, it was only – But my sisters were always critical of me: 'this is nonsense you are doing! You have no money'! and so forth. They were very critical of me.

Here, generation, as an objective structure, plays a crucial role. Amlang justifies the fact that his sister did not go to evening school by her poor school performance, but, most crucially, the idea that his sister would go to evening classes was unthinkable.

In Pellar's case, his sister, born in 1939, performed much better than he did in school, but the idea of her proceeding to evening school was still unthinkable. He said, 'And then my sister – she – actually – rather – I must say, she got only As. And nevertheless it was simply – there was, rather strange, this was no question at all. She stayed at home, so there wasn't any discussion that she might have learned something, yes, yes.' Pellar compared himself with this sister and his younger brother: 'first, I was rather lazy, so in elementary school and lower secondary school, I did only what had to be done, so in itself, this is certainly true, my sister got also a certificate, which – but she was rather ambitious, and even my brother, he was more well-behaved than me, he also got a better certificate than me, and my brother became finally a farmer, and my sister is, as I said – '

Pellar thought that his educational upward mobility could not be traced back to his school performance. Rather, the roles of his siblings were defined: his younger brother would inherit the farm, as was common in that area of Austria at the time, and, since his sister was a girl, no higher education was considered. Pellar's family saw higher education as possible only for boys. I asked whether, despite her good marks, it was clear that she would stay at home, and Pellar answered, 'She had to work with the horses in the field. No, that was, I mean, today it sounds, but there was such an attitude, sometimes a little bit conservative, it has to be said. But that – ' Pellar also had to get his work done while he studied, but his parents allowed him to try. His sister was denied that leeway.

A second key circumstance favoring men over women was the design of the evening school. First, that it was intended for men, not women, was explicitly stated at its establishment and remained so until 1940, when women were admitted. Second, either prior vocational education or a trade was considered for admittance. Both would be exceptional for women, as Amlang pointed out. Employment experience was another admission criterion that women found hard to meet, as they often worked in the home.

Finally, another institution that supported participation at an evening school, the *Kolpinghaus*, a low-cost boarding house, excluded women. The institution was founded by a priest to offer journeymen a home, and later offered a home to young men during their apprenticeships and, sometimes, education. During his studies at the evening school, Amlang stayed in a *Kolpinghaus* and reported that many fellow students did the same: 'Immediately got a spot, because it was very difficult to get into it, because there was a high demand, but the *Kolping* is the journeymen and employees and so on, many of them attended evening school during this time, so *Kolping* was the opportunity.'

In England, Finch, whose educational upward mobility was described in the section on socialization, also referred to his sister. Two years older than he, she also performed better at school; nevertheless, the milieu impeded her educational trajectory.

> She was academically bright, very bright, but I don't think she had any interest in the academic side. I say, she was reading Solzhenitsyn at the age of 13! But – also at the time – I think there was something there, and again in working-class backgrounds, you know, it was only really from – I think it's noticeable from probably from about my age, so people who are two years younger, well, you could see women actually coming up and saying. 'Actually I do want to go to university'; 'I do want to break the mold'. My sister, though, I think was more interested in having a good time than being academically bright. She wanted to have a good time, and therefore that meant you needed to get a job.

In contrast to his sister, Finch's educational career went straight up, possibly due to his good performance. In secondary school, he was in the top set and got five O levels. He transferred to the sixth form college and received three A levels. He enjoyed getting to know subjects, such as yoga, to which he would not have been exposed otherwise, and a world different from the one at home opened for him. When he was 18, in 1981, his father was laid off, and Finch realized that holding a job for life was no certainty. He started to view education differently. His father had huge difficulties in finding secure employment, rather than sequential temporary jobs, and Finch became engaged in Labour politics. He saw himself as useless at practical trades and decided to major in Peace Studies at a small, traditional university.

He fully enjoyed his life as a student, more in terms of engaging in politics than in academics, and received his BA (Hons.) in 1985. After graduation, he got a job locally and bought a house with his girlfriend. When the relationship broke up, he decided to change his career entirely and worked for a year in a hostel for homeless people. He realized that he wanted to do social work. In 1991, at the age of 27, he started a Master's in Applied Social Science and a diploma in Social Work on a full grant. Although independent from his parents, they still worried that he was renting again, while his siblings earned good wages. Again, he enjoyed his time as a student; however, this time, he was academically engaged. At the time of the interview, he was a commissioner, supporting people and adult care services. He characterized himself as middle class – cooking, baking bread, lovely wife, nice house – but many of his attitudes were still working class; for example, he worried about the widening inequalities in society.

The new in his life history was deeply embedded in his mother's middle-class origin and closely linked to a certain political stream in society during his youth: the 1980s peace movement and workers' protests against lay-offs under a Conservative government. Although he had clearly made the step from working to middle class, his profession expressed a continuity in his political attitudes, rooted in his working-class family's experiences.

4.7   Educational institutions for upward social mobility

One of the interviewees, Scott Johnson, studied at the Open University. In Austria, the *B-Matura*, an examination that enabled promotion to positions for which the highest school-leaving certificate was usually required, became a new option reserved for civil servants. This special chance was crucial in the life of Renate Steiner. The evening school in Austria was crucial in Moser's, Radler's, Amlang's, and Pellar's educational pathways. Here, I want to describe

Table 4.6   Interviewees who were educationally upwardly mobile due to specific educational institutions

Scott Johnson (male)	born 1960	in England	Mother: compulsory school; cleaner (ESeC: 9)
			Father: compulsory school; bank messenger (ESeC: 9)
Renate Steiner (female)	born 1954	in Austria	Mother: compulsory school; housewife (ESeC: 10)
			Father: compulsory school; bricklayer (ESeC: 8)
			Grandmother: went to a convent school, not clear for how long; house owner (ESeC: 10)
Georg Amlang (male)	born 1928	in Austria	Mother: no information on education; day laborer (453)
			Father: skilled carpenter; ill and unemployed (ISCED 453; ESeC 10)
Gerhard Moser (male)	born 1931	in Austria	Mother: compulsory school; housewife (ESeC 10)
			Father: skilled miller; steel worker (ESeC 9)
Erwin Radler (male)	born 1939	in Austria	Mother: compulsory school; household help, industrial worker (ESeC 9)
			Father: skilled scythe smith; partly captive (ISCED: 453; ESeC 8 and, temporarily, 10)
Hans Pellar (male)	born 1941	in Austria	Mother: probably compulsory school; farmer (ESeC 5)
			Father: probably compulsory school; farmer (ESeC 5)
Alexander Mair (male)	born 1966	in Austria	Parents' education and occupation unknown but ESeC 7 at highest
Friedrich Schrieben (male)	born 1966	in Austria	Mother: skilled shop assistant; waitress (ESeC 8)
			Father: skilled metal worker; train driver (ESeC 8)
Peter Mutz (male)	born 1960	in Austria	Mother: compulsory school; maidservant, agricultural laborer (ESeC 9)
			Father: skilled retail merchant; died young (ESeC 7)
Karin Eichner (female)	born 1972	in Austria	Mother: compulsory school; factory worker, cleaner, packer in retail (ESeC 9)
			Father: education unknown; taxi driver (ESeC 9)

the influence of these institutions in more detail and focus on another Austrian institution that enabled upward mobility: higher secondary vocational schools leading to the highest school-leaving certificate and therefore offering open access to tertiary education without subject-specific limitations. Mair and Schrieben show its importance; Peter Mutz earned his highest school-leaving certificate at an upper secondary vocational school, but other circumstances were more crucial for his educational upward mobility. Yet another educational institution enabled upward mobility: a university admission examination, which was accomplished by Karin Eichner.

4.7.1 England's Open University

Whether the Open University supports working-class inclusion is a subject of debate. One view regards this as the case, and, since it played a crucial role in the life of one educationally upwardly mobile interviewee, I list it as such without overlooking its shortcomings.

Scott Johnson studied at the Open University. We have already considered his educational upward mobility as being due to materially secure living conditions and his childhood lifestyle. We saw that his father supported him immensely by offering many educational opportunities, such as books. Born in 1960 to a cleaner and a bank messenger, Johnson went to a grammar school that became a comprehensive secondary school and then to a sixth form college in a county town. When he finished school, it was clear that he would go to university. He applied to Oxford to study mathematics and received a conditional offer. He stayed in college the night before his interview, and the bathroom was bigger than his whole house; he found the whole experience overwhelming and failed the interview.

He was then advised to avoid pure science in favor of engineering, which would provide more job opportunities. He enrolled in Electrical Engineering at another university in 1978, receiving a full grant that paid his fees and left him enough to live on. However, after a year, he realized that this course was wrong for him. He also had to move out of the residence hall and, in fact, out of the city to a place where he could afford to rent a room. He lost touch with fellow students. He struggled through his second year and, in the third, failed to complete his final year project and, therefore, the degree. He felt he had let his father down but said that his father took it much better than he had expected, quite rationally, without shouting.

Since Johnson had received a full maintenance grant, he could not receive another, so he took a job selling electronic components in a store for the next 20 years. He married, moved to another city, and, in 1987, became a father. Two years later, his second child was born, and he enrolled in the Open University. He was 30.

> I remember we bought my youngest one a desk, a little toy desk, and I don't quite know what made me decide I wanted to start to go to do university stuff. I think my job was – [sigh] – it numbed my brain. It paid the mortgage, and it was that sort of, you could get yourself trapped in a way; that you get yourself in a position with a company where they pay you, not a fortune, but they pay you enough to pay the mortgage. And you realize that if I want to get out of here I'm going to have to take a wage cut. And you've got a wife and two kids, mortgage – I can't afford to take a wage cut. Even though you know you're going to be earning more in the future, you're sort of trapped in there. So I was trapped in a job that – it was quite fun, but it wasn't demanding, and it didn't stimulate me greatly. But – So I decided that I needed to do something, and I think – I wasn't really aiming to get a degree and, but I've started it now, I just thought 'Why not? It'll be fun'. And in those days it wasn't expensive.

Johnson started at the Open University, mainly studying maths, but the courses were quite general in 1991.

The Open University began with Harold Wilson, prime minister of a Labour cabinet from 1964 to 1970 and 1974 to 1976, who was impressed by the large number of Soviet engineers who got their degrees by taking distance courses (MacArthur, 1974). Jennie Lee, minister of the arts in Wilson's first cabinet, played an important role. The literature on the Open University's founding emphasizes that Lee always wanted it to be recognized by its peers for not compromising academic standards (MacArthur, 1974; Rumble, 1982). According to Gemmeke (1983), five circumstances enabled realization of the Open University: a direct initiative of the minister, a prestigious planning committee, not spending on buildings and equipment, not informing the opposition, and no public discussion. The original aims were threefold: to improve education in general, to award degrees to hard-working students, and to reach students in other parts of the world (MacArthur, 1974). Rumble (1982) maintains that it did not refer to class directly but aimed to provide first and higher degree courses for adults who had been deprived of opportunities in the past. It was open to all adults with no requirement for a prior certificate or degree. It relied on the mass media to advertise courses, and admissions mainly followed the principle of first-come-first-served, but other factors were taken into account, such as regional and occupational quotas (Thomas, 1974).

At the beginning, most students were working in education and 70 per cent were men. Citing McIntosh and Calder, Rumble states that 'only a minority of Open University students appear "to have been genuinely disadvantaged at the *initial* level, i.e. not having been given the opportunity to study at a grammar or equivalent level school" ', and that they showed that the majority of Open University students (four out of five) had gone on to do some kind of post-school education as adults – either taking "further" or "adult" education courses, or teaching or some other vocational qualifications' (p. 56, emphasis original).

Johnson had both grammar school experience and post-school education. In fact, he fits the following description perfectly: 'The typical Open University student is a man, in his thirties, in a white-collar job; although he is now apparently middle class, his parents were probably working-class and he himself may well still call himself working-class. He has clearly already been involved in a lot of study, either "full" or "part-time", and thus has been able to move on to a job from his parents' (McIntosh, 1974, p. 54). Johnson worked hard and completed half a course more than part-time students usually did, but then his company was sold, and the atmosphere changed from friendly to anonymous and exploitative. Colleagues who left were not replaced; staff turnover was high, so the workload increased tremendously. Johnson could not continue his studies, but was allowed to keep the books.

> And that was it. I sort of gave up on thoughts of continuing it for a little while; I thought, well, maybe one day I'll be able to pick it up, because the nice thing about the Open U is they don't care if you take 25 years over a degree. [laughs]. I achieved nearly enough units to pass a degree I thought, but not enough units for honors. ... I think I had this idea that I'd been going on for it, that I was going to get this degree and then, hopefully, our

money situation would be all right for a year while I did a Teacher Training Course...'

Johnson was unable to continue for a very long time. His immediate boss had a complete breakdown, and Johnson had to work seven days a week and evenings. His third child was born. His father died before Johnson was able to see him because of the work, and Johnson suffered a severe bout of depression and was let go. The next year, his mother died.

Johnson inherited £80,000 and used it to go back to the Open University, finish a BA in 2005 and complete a foundation course at a Russell Group university the following year. From 2006 to 2009, he studied maths and received his BSc Hons. He won funding to conduct an eight-week summer project and loved the work, which led him to think about pursuing a PhD. He presented a proposal on general relativity, and, though he was initially turned down for a grant, when another student dropped out a member of staff modified the project to make it more applied, and Johnson got a fast-track scholarship that allowed him to do his PhD without having a Master's. He aimed to finish in four years.

It seems that the Open University played an ambivalent role in Johnson's educational path, which could be argued to lie within the ambivalent character of the Open University in relation to supporting working-class people. On the one hand, the Open University provided Johnson with an intellectual challenge and thus formed a counterweight to his boring work. On the other hand, due to his work, he was unable to study properly and to complete his degree in a reasonable time. Rumble (1982) refers to Lewis, who was warning that the Open University was likely to be 'yet another university institution for the middle-class' (Lewis cited by Rumble 1982: 12). In his estimation of the Open University's contribution to educational reform, Gemmeke (1983) comments critically that the fact that people working full-time were allowed to study was also an economic calculation of avoiding a shortage of workforce in the labor markets. Gemmeke holds that the Open University combined individual catching up with the economic need for a highly qualified workforce, but that no structural change was intended or achieved. Through open admission, the practice of admission following prior degrees, certificates, and marks of other universities was abolished. Apart from this, traditional academic values have not been touched.

4.7.2 *B-Matura* and evening school in Austria

In the life of Renate Steiner, two educational institutions supporting atypical pathways played a key role: the *B-Matura*, the highest school-leaving certificate offered exclusively to allow civil servants to move up in their ranking, and the evening school already mentioned in Amlang's and Pellar's lives. The *B-Matura* gave Steiner the self-confidence to go for the complete *Matura*, the highest school-leaving certificate (ISCED 344) in Austria, which enabled her to study law.

Steiner was born in 1954 in a small village close to a large city in upper Austria. Her mother was 23 years old and forced to marry because of the pregnancy. She finished compulsory school in eight years and worked as a housewife. Steiner's father was 30 years old and a bricklayer but not educated as a master builder. When he was 20, he was adopted by his stepmother, who came from a bourgeois family in Vienna and owned various properties. His biological mother never married and was not taking care of her son at the time of his adoption. His father worked for a farmer, taking care of the horses, and later worked as a paver. Steiner's parents and paternal grandparents lived in a two-family house owned by her grandmother. Steiner lived with her grandparents downstairs, and her parents and four younger siblings lived upstairs.

Thus, her family's social milieu was not homogeneous. While her parents were clearly working class, her grandmother, with whom Steiner stayed until she was 15, was not. Before she started school, she went with her grandparents every day to a coffee house, where they read the papers. According to Steiner, her grandmother was the first woman in upper Austria to file and to win lawsuits because of 'Hitler issues'. She was the sole owner of various properties and described as a person of authority.

During her first two years, Steiner was often very ill and stayed for long periods in hospital. When she was six, she started to suffer from asthma, and she remained very delicate until she was 12. At six, she also started at an elementary school within walking distance. By then, she had two younger sisters. She recalled that she had read more books than her classmates, but she had to repeat a year because of long absences due to illness. Steiner continued on to lower secondary school (*Hauptschule*) in the city nearby. Her first brother was born and welcomed as the first male child; two years later, a second brother arrived. In her last year of *Hauptschule*, in 1969, the headmaster visited her parents to ask them to allow their daughter to continue on to upper secondary school, but her father did not want to pay 50 Groschen for the bus, and her mother did not care. Steiner said that her parents had no confidence that she would be able to reach the highest school-leaving certificate and did not want to invest money in the education of a girl. She described them as ignorant in relation to intrinsic education. Her grandmother was in favor of more schooling, but did not interfere.

A career counsellor visited the lower secondary school, allocating apprentices to firms who needed them. Two weeks after she finished compulsory school, Steiner started as a retail apprentice in a store selling paper, leather goods, and toys. For three years, her vocational education combined workplace learning and one or two days a week of vocational school. Apprentices in this dual system earned a small salary. When she began, Steiner got her own room on the upper floor and lived with her parents and siblings.

After finishing her vocational education, she worked for the obligatory period at the shop and taught herself stenography so that she would later be able to work in an office. In 1973, the age of legal majority was reduced from 21 to 19, and Steiner moved out of her home and rented her own room in the city, where she worked as a secretary in the federal state hospital. She earned less, but her employment was permanent. She kept taking classes and passed several exams.

A year later, Steiner started the *B-Matura*, an educational path that was replaced in 2009 by the *Berufsreifeprüfung*, a university-access exam for people who were vocationally educated and had vocational experience without having obtained the highest school-leaving certificate. The *B* in *B-Matura* stands for *Beamte*, or civil servants, and it enabled civil servants to access well-paying upper positions in public service without the generally compulsory highest school-leaving certificate. Steiner assessed its impact: 'I was one of the best, and this gave me so much self-confidence that I started – so I really earned the highest school-leaving certificate.'

Unfortunately, there are no official statistics on the numbers of *B-Matura* awarded, so it is difficult to estimate its effect on civil servants in Austria. Over five semesters, three evenings a week, students were taught the content of the first four years of upper secondary school. In the end, there was a commissioned examination of all subjects. Straight after Steiner passed it with among the highest marks, she was promoted, and she started evening school, then called *Arbeitermittelschule*, and studied for the highest school-leaving certificate from 1976 to 1981.

The evening school was a product of the Austrian First Republic and, more specifically, the law for secondary schools passed under a conservative government in 1927. The first cohort at Steiner's school started in 1928 with 45 students, of whom 14 passed the final exam in 1932 (Absolventenverband, n.d.). Male students who had finished compulsory school and passed either a vocational education or their 17th birthday or had worked were allowed to attend. For five evenings, from 18:00 to 22:30 (later 22:00), male teachers taught the upper secondary school curriculum. In 1934, a government decree recognized the evening school as a special school. In 1940, women were allowed to attend, and in 1942, due to the war, women were allowed to teach. From April to September 1945, evening schools were closed, and when they reopened their legal status was not completely clear. Five years later, in 1950, a decree of the education ministry based on the law of 1927 regulated evening schools, which were not part of the school law. A new rule established student self-administration. In 1962, evening schools received some additional regulations based on parts of the school law. Only in 1988 was a comprehensive law set up for all evening schools, and in 1997 a specific law was set up for employed students, whose interests had not been represented.

Until the mid-1980s – thus, during Steiner's tenure – minor subjects were completed one after another, so the final semester exclusively addressed the main subjects. All students except those employed in public service could apply for a grant to support the last semester at the local *Arbeiterkammer*, the group that represented employee interests from 1969 onward.

In 1971, Steiner's evening school had the highest number of students, at 692 (Rohringer, n.d.). While in the past most teachers had been employed by the school (in 1963, 83 per cent, who taught 93 per cent of classes), later they were employed at other schools as well, teaching only modules and not whole cohorts from entry to their degrees. Consequently, the atmosphere became less personal.

The social composition of the student body also changed. From 1963 to 1968, half came from lower social backgrounds (Absolventenverband, n.d., p. 71), but a 1977 study of graduates in Linz revealed the last occupation before starting evening school: 57 per cent self-employed artisans, skilled workers, lower employees, housewives, and pupils; 34 per cent semi-skilled and employed workers and small farmers; and 4 per cent unskilled workers (Jaroschka, 1999, p. 75). Compared with 90 per cent in 1945, only 75 per cent of the student body came from manual professions. In the winter term of 1987–8, the number of female students peaked at 51 per cent, compared with about 35 per cent in the summer term of 1978. According to Vogl (n.d.), in 1981, when Steiner graduated, the success rate was 24 per cent, although 95 per cent of students who took the exams passed, and 41 per cent obtained the best mark. Most were Catholics and almost all Austrians. Most were 24 years old and unmarried.

Steiner described daily life during her years at the evening school:

> Back then at the evening school, four and a half hours or five hours of sleep was enough and that for five years, because I have – there were classes until 10 P.M., and by the time I got home, it was about 11 P.M., then I studied a bit more, I mean, I couldn't learn so late, but at least I wrote something down or prepared something, and then it was midnight, and in the early morning, I got to my office, yes, was – yes, I mean one learns how to schedule time, because study time was in my case in the early mornings, that was when I could learn best, yes.

She gained self-confidence and explained its significance: 'The evening school was really the starting point for real-life education, the kind that opens doors – yes, it was so real – when I obtained the highest school-leaving certificate, and I knew, so now I can really choose whether I want to do something more and if so, what interests me, now I can choose what I am interested in, and all doors are open to me.'

The evening school led to the highest school-leaving certificate, the *Matura*, a name that suggests having the maturity to study autonomously in the university. Steiner was not restricted to a particular subject or program close to her employment area but could choose any course from Arabic to zoology, and she seems to have developed a wide range of interests *at* the evening school, which would have been impossible without the general education she received there. She learned ancient Greek and Latin and developed a special interest and joy in ancient Greek. She thought about becoming a classical philologist but opted for law, as it required some Latin and was offered at the university close to her home and workplace.

Two years later, she married and bore her first daughter. The new family moved to a village and took on a mortgage. Steiner had to remain employed full-time to contribute to mortgage payments, and she also lacked a driving license, which might have allowed her to commute to school in a car. Two years later, her second daughter was born, and two years later, a third. She wanted to continue her studies, but her husband was against it. Eventually, they divorced, and Steiner picked up her studies 12 years after she had started, but, after two years of studying, working, and raising her three daughters alone, she dropped out a second time for two years. From 1997 to 2007, she studied part-time and worked full-time and also obtained various vocational qualifications. At the time of the interview, she was working on her PhD thesis.

To identify the new in Steiner's life history is rather complicated because she came from a heterogeneous milieu. First, she lived with her upper-class grandmother for her first 15 years, but her grandmother did not have a strong influence on her or support her formal education, and her parents sent her to inferior institutions. In fact, the crucial step enabling something new was her departure from home. She left as soon as she was legally allowed and in a planned, rather 'cool' way, without discussion, moving out and into her own flat from one day to the next. She remained distant from her original family and, in contrast to other interviewees' lives, social change was embedded in her original milieu only in the sense that she separated from it: specifically, from parents who provided no encouragement or support. During her life, the new was realized through her own enormous efforts: seemingly endless further education while working and raising three children as a single parent.

Four other interviewees (Amlang, Moser, Radler, and Pellar) achieved their highest school-leaving degree at the evening school, but, since other circumstances played more decisive roles, I have reported on their lives under other headings.

4.7.3 Upper secondary vocational schools providing direct and comprehensive access to higher education

Austria has a special educational institution, the upper secondary vocational school, which extends from grade nine to grade twelve and offers both a vocational education with a diploma and a more general education. Although mainly intended for such applications as profession-specific English or applied mathematics, it awards the highest school-leaving certificate (ISCED 354), thus opening the gate to all university subjects. It runs five years, one year longer than traditional upper secondary schools. The main types support the technical and commercial professions, but there are also schools for tourism, fashion, early childhood pedagogy, domestic economy, agriculture, and forestry. Gender is highly imbalanced; in 2003–4, women comprised only 4.8 per cent of the student population, while at commercial schools the share is more equal, with 45.6 per cent men (Schlögl, 2007).

Both types of upper secondary vocational schools have a long tradition, dating back to the government (1740–80) of Maria Theresia, who established a determined mercantile policy (Schaeren, 1989). They dissolved the division between academic (general) and vocational education in Austria, which is quite different from England, where vocational subjects are offered at the tertiary level to a much larger extent. In 1920, the Austrian Ministry of Education granted upper secondary commercial schools the right to grant the highest school-leaving certificate; admission is open to all students who finish compulsory school, and the screening test is not very selective (Schaeren, 1989). In terms of entrance, most students continue from lower secondary school, but a relevant proportion (about 25 per cent at the end of 1970s) enter from upper secondary general schools after finishing grade four (Grüner, 1980).

In 2005, about 37 per cent of upper secondary commercial school graduates studied at universities (about 11.3 per cent at universities of applied sciences), about 69 per cent were employed, and some both studied and worked. While in 1983–4 the share of tenth-grade students in both upper secondary commercial and technical schools was 6.7 per cent, this similarity changed; in 2006–7, 10.2 per cent studied in technical schools and 7.9 per cent in commercial schools. Upper commercial schools seem to lead to employment most securely: according to the 2001 census, only 3.2 per cent of their graduates were unemployed as compared with 5.4 per cent of graduates from general upper secondary schools (Schneeberger & Nowak, 2010). In addition to offering very good prospects for future employment, upper secondary vocational schools were seen as more accessible than general upper secondary schools, with more academically oriented subjects, by many interviewees and their parents. However, the good prospects for employment could be interpreted as a way of diverting people from pursuing higher education.

In addition to Schrieben and Mair, Mutz earned his highest school-leaving certificate at an upper vocational school, but his educational upward mobility may be better explained by a certain kind of coping within emotionally precarious social contexts. Schrieben and Mair were both portrayed in the section on socialization, which I consider their main enabling circumstance, but we have acknowledged that all socially upward trajectories require a number of sometimes inter-relating circumstances and conditions.

Both men were born in 1966, and their parents endeavored to enable good educational conditions. Both went from *Hauptschule* to upper secondary vocational schools and graduated with the highest school-leaving certificate. While Schrieben worked for a couple of years afterward, Mair went directly to university. They both perceived the upper secondary vocational school as somewhat more accessible, familiar, and sensible than the traditional upper secondary general school.

Schrieben had a brother two years his senior who went to a technical upper secondary vocational school, while Schrieben opted for a commercial one. He said, 'four colleagues from the Hauptschule just went to [city] to the HAK [acronym for *Handelsakademie*, or upper commercial secondary school], so now I did the same of course, about like that, yes'. Three of these classmates were girls, daughters of small farmers, and one was the son of a businessman. No classmate went to an upper secondary general school.

Schrieben went on to describe how some teachers at his very traditional *Hauptschule* were old-fashioned and treated the pupils badly. In his tenth year (third grade), he failed two subjects and had to study over the summer, so he could repeat and pass examinations at the beginning of the new school year; otherwise, he would have had to repeat the whole year, which is the rule in Austria. However, throughout his five years, he enjoyed, got along with, and felt protected by one particular teacher. Apart from the four classmates who decided to continue on to the upper secondary commercial school, Schrieben had another reason for choosing it over an upper secondary general school: 'what was important for security was this *vocational* education, that this was not a *Gymnasium*, but a vocational upper school, you had a profession when you finished it, that was certainly a major factor, too, I can remember, in the decision'. I asked him whether the vocational aspect was crucial for him and/ or for his parents, and he said: 'Ah, for me and as one factor for my parents, then, too, so, so that, it was easy, like a typical father, no, father, so these career thoughts of the son's, no, well, "if you do the HAK now, this is a prerequisite for or a kind of basis for a profitable career perhaps, more than you might have perhaps in a *Gymnasium*", because at that time, there was no idea of studying at a university at all'. He described his parents' attitude as embedded, reflecting the attitudes and ways of thinking of their class and the social milieu of the time:

> So, the idea of a career, well, then he goes to university after the *Gymnasium*, that was certainly, still, as far as my parents – and just – because that was a complete blank to you. University, all this – by the time they found out what enrolling and what were else, all this, how it works at the university and so on, it was always more or less Greek to them, you might say. So, for this reason...I mean, not to underestimate it, but it was then, well, in the 1970s, the idea of a highly educated professional simply did not exist, no, but there was, ok, HTL [*Höhere Technische Lehranstalt*], HAK, these were the levels that were aspired to for the children, no, and beyond that, going to work vocationally. So even higher education, this was, I believe, I mean, perhaps I do them an injustice now, my mother certainly, but my father, whether he thought about the future, that they might be able to

study, perhaps, he might have thought of it, but in the sense that he would have presented it as a possibility to us, it was certainly not in that way.

After Schrieben finished the upper secondary vocational school, he worked for five and a half years in a bank but did not feel comfortable there. Having worked for such a long period qualified him to receive the highest grant to study at a university, which he did. I asked him how he started a course of study, and, after a long pause, he answered:

> Partly, certainly, it was that our class teacher in the HAK said, 'If you are going to study some day, so because you all have done HAK, you would not have any problems at university.' He made some references to business administration, was certainly partly a factor, so that I – so then I always – of course, I had colleagues who came to university from the HAK, where I thought, well, good, he was not much better in HAK, and now he is an educated professional, so looking at it that way, it might be a possibility.

Once he decided to study, he thought he would study business administration because of his vocational education, but at the Student Advisory Service he met a friend who convinced him within ten minutes to study social economy. Schrieben's upward mobility was a gradual process of entering new territories that were closely linked to familiar elements like his parents' attitudes, his classmates' paths, the subject content, and a friend's advice. The educational institution played a key role, offering both a vocational degree enabling access to employment and the highest school-leaving degree, opening the door to university with all its subjects. The institution was something new and introduced social change, as Schrieben's parents both held vocational but not academic degrees, so his educational upward mobility was linked to their vocational education, but went beyond to higher education through his attendance at the upper secondary vocational school.

Another example of gradual educational upward mobility is Mair's life history. He, too, went to an upper secondary vocational school after completing the compulsory *Hauptschule*, but he opted for a technical school. He described the transition:

And I can't, to be honest, remember exactly why I then went to HTL, but [laughs] I believe that it was also my parents' influence there, they, actually, yes, at least, I don't know, at least they presented it very positively and probably [laughs] that I would not do an apprenticeship, but actually, in a, yes, going on to a school, that was actually already clear, yes, or actually earlier, still earlier perhaps already while *Hauptschule* in the third, so at least in the third year, I believe, but why now an HTL and not an AHS [*Allgemeinbildende Höhere Schule*], I can't say now. [laughs] I mean, it depends perhaps, as I said, influenced a bit probably by my parents and also because of the better future prospects or what, if one does a HTL, because one simply has – a completed vocational education does take a year longer, but it gives you a degree with which you can start something unlike going into an AHS. That was probably also a reason.

In contrast to Schrieben, Mair began his studies immediately after finishing upper technical school. He said he started to think about studying in the fourth or fifth year, as the topic was discussed at school. Together with friends, he went to a university that was highly recommended by one of their teachers. They obtained places in the dorms, and Mair shared a room for the next four years, then moved to private accommodation for two years. After graduation, he was employed by a company for which he had worked in summer jobs and internships. He was still working there at the time of the interview.

His educational and social rise was still gradual, closely linked to his parents' and classmates' attitudes and actions. The upper secondary vocational school was new but embedded in his milieu of immense constancy because, by combining vocational and academic education, it represented no risk. As a good student, he was unlikely to face academic difficulties or later unemployment. His transition to university was secure: advised by a favorite teacher, accompanied by five classmates, and sharing a room with two of them for the unfamiliar first years. Each of Mair's steps led him to something new, but in a reassuring context.

4.7.4 Study authorization examination

The study authorization examination (*Studienberechtigungsprüfung*) is an inclusive instrument in the Austrian educational system, dating back to 1939 (Schlögl, 2007). It aims to offer people who do not obtain the highest school-leaving certificate access to a university or a university of applied sciences. However, access is limited to certain study subjects, in contrast to the professional maturity examination (*Berufsreifeprüfung*), introduced in 1997, which is restricted to people with a vocational degree, but, once they pass, they can study any subject they choose.

The study authorization examination is regarded as part of university study, as evidenced by eligibility for grant support (Schlögl, 2007). Students must be Austrian citizens or legal residents; must be at least 22 years old, or 20 if they can provide evidence of having completed compulsory school and at least four years of vocational education; and must have decided to study a specific subject. Since 1998–9, the number of people passing the examination has decreased, probably due to the introduction of the professional maturity examination in 1997. In 1994–5, the year interviewee Karin Eichner took it, 1,154 study authorization examinations were taken, 49.7 per cent by women. In 2001–2, the number fell to 588, but 54.1 per cent were women (Schlögl, 2007).

Karin Eichner was born in 1972. She studied at *Hauptschule* and a commercial upper secondary vocational school but left after two years with a medium degree. She took an apprenticeship, employment, and, in 1994, the study authorization examination. She decided to study social economics: 'Yes, I took the entrance authorization examination, had – I learned mostly by myself, took two courses in maths and in English and that too was, yes, it was nice to learn again; it was fun, and it wasn't terribly difficult, so it is – it went fine, and after work – I have always worked a lot, have done that alongside, and it went well.'

Eichner had to pass exams in four subjects in addition to maths and English: German, history, geography, and social studies. She received study materials for German, history, and geography from the university and did not participate in the university course offered because she had to work. She had not yet been offered a study grant, but, since she knew she could receive one once she enrolled in university, based on her former employment and independently of her parents, she worked exactly four years, the time required for grant eligibility, and began study in the winter term of 1995. I will come back to her in the following section.

4.8 Seeking truth in higher education as a process of educational upward mobility

Education has psychological dimensions. Human beings have bodies and minds, and we are social beings, living together. In Chapter 1, we noted research findings on the psychological difficulties of educational upward mobility: ambivalence, alienation, loss, and pain. However, educational upward mobility can also be a way out of socially and emotionally precarious family constellations to achieve social and emotional security. This section focuses on the mental dimensions of the social. Bourdieu's concept of habitus captures such mental dimensions as perceptions, attitudes, logic, and emotions, and he emphasizes the functional contribution of unconsciousness to perpetuating social hierarchies. This dimension is often overlooked, although it deepens our understanding of social processes. In contrast to Walkerdine et al. (2001, p. 95), who consider the psychological area a limit to sociological research, I intend to demonstrate how far Bourdieu's conceptual framework allows us to analyze and to argue, something he himself did not exploit to its full potential. This section will examine how certain social situations are perceived and how coping with difficult experiences can lead, along with concrete material social conditions, to educational upward mobility. In the life histories I relate, educational upward mobility required concrete material conditions that still cannot be separated from the mental effects of social situations in childhood. I do not mean that minds are a given part of social descriptions, but that *mind is important for educational upward mobility under special social circumstances.*

This section is structured in two parts. First, I will discuss three life histories in which emotionally precarious childhoods led to educational upward mobility. Second, I will consider the relationship of truth to security and/or comfort, or a certain understanding and dimension of education in relation to specific types of social situations and specific ways of coping with them.

4.8.1 Emotionally precarious social contexts and mental coping

The interviewees who sought higher education in order to cope with great upheavals, abandonment, and neglect are listed in Table 4.7.

Table 4.7 Interviewees whose studies in higher education helped them to overcome the emotionally precarious social contexts they experienced in childhood

Peter Mutz	born in 1960	Austria	Mother: compulsory school; maidservant, farm worker (ESeC 9)
			Father: skilled retail merchant, died early (ESeC 7)
Oliver Berry	born in 1960	England	Mother: education and occupation unknown
			Father: education unknown, lorry driver, works in a pub (ESeC 9)
Karin Eichner	born in 1972	Austria	Mother: compulsory school; factory worker, cleaner, packer in retail (ESeC 9)
			Father: education unknown; taxi driver (ESeC 9)

4.8.1.1 Abandonment overcome by a logical viewpoint acquired from higher education

Peter Mutz was born in a small village in upper Austria in 1960. His mother was 29, from a rural area, and left school at the end of compulsory education, although she had wanted to become a teacher. Instead, she worked as a maid. Mutz's father was 31, also from a rural area, where he worked as a farm hand after achieving a compulsory school-leaving degree. Later, he apprenticed to a retail merchant and became one himself. The family also ran a small farm. Mutz was the youngest of four children; his two brothers were seven and two years older, and his sister five years older. During his early childhood, his parents ran their own shop and built a very large house. Mutz started at a local kindergarten at the age of five and primary school at six. In his first year of primary school, however, his life was shaken to the foundations: his father committed suicide. Mutz never mentioned a reason and avoided talking about it, but I had the impression that he attributed it to large debts. Only in the second part of the interview did he mention his father's suicide.

I mean, the beginning of school is my father – The suicide was naturally an insanity at home, no, everything was shattered, and he kept a shop, and back then it was usual that the wives, they donated their services, you didn't employ them, that would have cost taxes, which my mother nowadays regrets in her pension. No, in those days, you bought a shop in life annuity, and there was a giant mountain of debt, and she doesn't know any accounting or anything, no, has always worked quite a lot and has taken this over, and that was insane at the time – that is actually something one does not want to experience as a child, and then coming to boarding school, that was even – In this school, I actually did not feel so badly, but this loss [*Verlorenheit*], that was simply there, no, so certain things you have to learn later, for example that you – we went to bed with dirty feet in the summers because mother had no time. The shop was open 40 hours or so, four kids, a household, and in the evening, she needed to do the accounting or something – we grew up like savages, no, and these are things you regret later, not regret, but have to learn later. If you have education, you know you don't have to smell, or you need to change your underwear or whatever [laughs], brush your teeth [laughs], but that is, those were a bit more savage times.

Clearly, his mother's situation made excessive demands on her: suddenly a widow with four children, running a shop without the necessary training and with large debts. As a result, the children grew up unsupervised, but Mutz did not enjoy his freedom; to material neglect was added emotional neglect because his father had abandoned him.

In Austria, elementary school takes four years, and, afterward, pupils usually continue to either *Hauptschule* or *Allgemeine Höhere Schule*. In rural areas, the *Hauptschule* was often the only option and often provided an education comparable to the second option, the higher level of secondary schools. Mutz went to a Catholic boarding school where his two brothers were already enrolled, due partly, he thought, to the precarious conditions at home after his father's death; partly to his mother's strong affinity for education, which she had had since childhood, when becoming a teacher was out of her reach; and partly to the impossibility of commuting to the nearest *Gymnasium*. The boarding school was run by a congregation of priests who emphasized foreign missions. They treated Mutz violently: 'They had a brother who was very, very, very brutal. What do you call brutal? He was also extremely strict and then there was corporal punishment. This was in the late 1960s, early 1970s, a totally normal instrument of education in Austria. Receiving a slap in the face from the priest was something normal, no, nobody complained. You were immediately so ashamed that you didn't tell at home, no.'

Apart from religious education, the boarding school offered general education leading to the highest school-leaving certificate. From an early age, then, Mutz was educated to obtain the highest school-leaving certificate and to study at a university. Having a goal is important for long higher educational pathways. Mutz was allowed to go home on weekends every two or three weeks. He felt dreadful at school, and during his third year he stopped working and was expelled. He was 13 years old and switched to the *Hauptschule* in his home village, which meant coming back home. One of his older brothers had already switched. At this time, his mother closed the shop and had more time for her children, a material condition that allowed him to live at home. Over the next 15 years, she planted strawberries; Mutz and his siblings assisted during the summer. She later became a cook in a canteen.

At the same time, Mutz's paternal uncle became a psychological parent and father substitute. He was a Social Democrat, and Mutz admired his social and political work in an area dominated by the Conservatives. He also ran the local newspaper, where Mutz helped as a binder and engaged socially, playing cards in the evening with the other men. In contrast, his mother, as a widow, was stripped of social contacts apart from work.

After a year and a half, Mutz finished *Hauptschule*. The School Act of 1962 prolonged compulsory school from eight to nine years, and, since *Hauptschule* has only eight grades, career counsellors come to schools to advise pupils about their subsequent options. Such counsellors apprised Mutz of a recently opened *Höhere Technische Lehranstalt*, an upper secondary school that offered vocational education and the highest school-leaving certificate. It had courses in hotel management, and Mutz was interested:

> Well, so hotel management and things like that, I already had at six. I told the people that I – a six-year-old normally is not allowed to touch the stove, and we had a gas stove – I could prepare a noodle soup at six. I naturally said that I can cook. By the way, I am – in school, obviously, I wasn't interested in cooking until then in this hotel management school, because boys have other

interests than cooking, but I am a very enthusiastic cook at home in our family.

Mutz had no other plans or concrete ideas about what he was going to do, so he went away from home to hotel management school for five years in a stream leading to the highest school-leaving certificate. He lived in the boarding school for the first two years and, when he was about 16, rented a room. His bond to his home village dissolved, and his friendships were elsewhere.

In 1979, at the age of 19, Mutz finished school with a vocational education and the highest school-leaving certificate. He immediately started his military service. He would have preferred alternative civilian service, but he would have had to wait for a place, and his mother wanted him to serve immediately, arguing that military service enhanced job prospects. He was sent to a remote barracks and, after finishing, started work as a receptionist in a sports hotel for six months during the summer season. He went on to work in a travel agency for three years and was promoted quickly because of gender preference.

During this time, he moved back into his mother's large house but participated in an alternative, left-wing scene that met at a cultural center founded in the late 1970s in a nearby town. Most of his friends were part of it. He started riding a motor bike on long tours around Europe. Many of his friends were at university, so Mutz began thinking about studying as well. His sister was earning a salary as a teacher and offered to fund his studies, but Mutz wanted to be financially autonomous and refused. The catalyst for his decision to go to university was an irrational act of pettiness by his boss. Although offered a promotion, he turned it down and left to study business administration, then switched quickly to sociology and, later, economics, as he found sociology boring, and the economics faculty was highly regarded. Mutz was eligible for a full study grant. He shared a flat for a year and a half, but the community was ousted when the owner wanted the flat for himself. Mutz and his girlfriend moved into a small apartment in a student dorm run by the Social Democrats. Here, contacts made through his uncle were helpful.

Mutz enjoyed studying. He talked enthusiastically in detail about lectures and professors. More generally: 'I never had difficulty learning, especially when it was related to maths or formulas. I surprise my son when we learn maths together, I always do well. This is much more interesting than all the other stuff you need to learn by heart. Maths is pure logic, this is absolutely interesting.' As for economics: 'Economics was interesting because I liked maths and logical things. Let's say that model stuff, I like very much, right? And those graphs and formulas made me very happy, something others are often annoyed by [laughs]. Other people can't stand that, this theorizing. It is terrible that I became a practitioner because I was always in love with theory.' He explained why he wanted to be a practitioner:

> It was always important to me to be simply able to do many things, not being able to rely on someone, but this is due to my biography, because having been abandoned or in distress, I often wished as a 17, 18 year-old that I was grown up, because then I could take matters into my own hands...that is this helplessness that I felt perhaps in my childhood, right? That one needs to be able to do things, to fight one's way through.

When Mutz was about 26, some state funds ran out, and he had to get a job. After five years, the full study grant also ended. He was engaged by a self-governing association for work and education and replaced someone in the state-run job center for a year. He suffered by not finishing his studies, but he had to work. Finally, he agreed to write his Master's dissertation on widening participation in vocational education and lived on unemployment compensation. After a total seven years of studying, the last two part-time, he finished at the age of 30. His dissertation won a prestigious award.

He was hired by a research institute, but was swamped and resigned. He began to work in the social area, where he earned much less but felt well. At the age of 37, he became a father and now lives with his partner and three children.

Mutz's existential need was to be a practitioner, autonomous, because he could not rely on anyone. From higher education, he sought realization, knowledge, and logic – the calculable. Knowing where something leads provides security and, for Mutz, satisfaction. Summarizing the emergence of the new in his life history, once again, it was founded in the family. His mother had a high appreciation of education, supported by her own mother, who died early. She sent her sons to a Catholic boarding school where they could achieve the highest school-leaving certificate. Mutz's father was modern; he was skiing in the 1950s. The social-democratic tradition in his family, embodied by his uncle, created an open mind and attitude about the world. It led Mutz to the cultural center, where he met many young people who had obtained the highest school-leaving certificate and brought new art, music, lifestyles, and political consciousness to a rural area generally dominated by brass bands and voluntary fire brigades, where young people are introduced to drinking large amounts of alcohol.

The new in Mutz's life was also related to leaving the village, first, to the boarding school at the age of 10, and, second, at 14, to an upper secondary vocational boarding school. Both schools offered the highest school-leaving certificate, so he developed a long-term perspective that encompassed higher education and was surrounded by classmates who were more likely to come from middle-class than working-class families. Mutz was not the only member of his family who studied; although the brother who studied did not finish, his sister fulfilled their mother's ambition to become a teacher. Another possible reason for leaving his milieu might be his father's suicide: at home, he had no positive role model but, rather, a dreadful memory.

Overall, Mutz's path was embedded in his original social-democratic milieu and the later, more left-wing/alternative scene he engaged in. He secured his flat through social-democratic connections, and chose a profession that allowed him to work toward social change.

4.8.1.2　*Higher education providing orientation after great upheavals in childhood*

Oliver Berry was also born in 1960, in a small town north of London. He estimated that his mother must have been about 19 when his sister was born and 21 when he was born. Berry did not know his father's age, either, but both parents finished compulsory school at 14 and had no further education. Berry's father worked for his own father, delivering market garden produce to London, and the grandfather gave Berry's family a house. The father's younger brother was qualified as an accountant. When Berry was two years old, his father left the family. He came home with his mother and sister, and they found out that his father was gone: 'we had no keys to get into the house and realized that father had gone. Well, I was 2 and a half, yeah. So father not around any more. Um – and so ok, what happens, you know, mother kind of had a nervous breakdown.' Later in the interview, he returned to this scene: 'And my memory of that house is having to climb through one of the small windows on the day we arrived back. We couldn't have the – we couldn't find the keys. The window was open, so I had to climb through and then get a chair, a big chair. Stand at the door, and undo the door from inside to let my mother and my sister in.'

His mother's nervous breakdown lasted a while, so Berry and his sister became wards of the court and were about to be sent to an orphanage when his paternal grandparents took them in. They owned 100 acres and several houses, which they rented and poured the receipts back into their market gardening business. Berry did not remember whether his grandfather inherited money or built the business from a small parcel of land, but he believed the latter. He only found out about the houses after his grandparents died. They belonged to the Methodist Church and were very religious, especially the grandmother. Life with them was stable and enjoyable. Berry emphasized that he grew up with certain values, such as being generous, helpful, and not interfering in other people's business. He went to Sunday school with his grandparents and celebrated the harvest with suppers in September. He had a lot of freedom on the farm and learned to drive a tractor. Seasonal changes and the process of growing things were integral to his background. When I asked him to tell me about daily life during this time, he said:

You kind of walk down the farm with your grandfather. He was effectively your father at that particular point in time, and you kind of see things in there – was dogs chained up, because that's what you had on a farm when there was machinery around and there was growth, there was planting, there was watering, irrigation systems. I remember those; they used to have a stream, and it always used to get the fresh water to put on the land from the stream. There was a pump with gasoline in it. They had [hesitates] a mobile home in the – a caravanette? I don't know what type of words you would use in, in, um, German to describe it, but um [hesitates], yeah, so sometimes we used to go away on holiday for long weekends in the caravanette. S. and B., that's northeast coast, being two places where they liked to go. Um [hesitates], but they're always, they always seemed loving and, and, trying to undertake the role of the parent.

When Berry was about seven years old, his father returned with a woman and her two daughters, and they all moved back into the house where they had lived before. The father returned to working for his parents on the farm. Berry remembered being the usher at his father's wedding.

At the same time, his mother had another nervous breakdown but then married, and Berry and his sister were allowed to visit her every other Sunday. His mother and stepfather had a son and a daughter together, but the husband was violent toward Berry and his sister, and the visits stopped. From this time until Berry was 22, he had no contact with his mother. He said: 'My mother eventually did leave my second father during that period as well. And she went to live on a houseboat – a wooden boat – but he found her, and he set fire to the – set fire to the wooden house. And, hence, he was sent to prison for arson, blah, blah, blah. Yeah, yeah. But it left some [pause] deep emotional kind of scars.'

In infant school, Berry's class had to participate in intelligence tests every two weeks over a two-year period. According to Berry, the pupils had to answer 20 questions in 60 seconds. Only he and one other pupil regularly answered 18–20 questions: 'So the rest of the people in the class had started to build up this kind of like, "Ok, Ok, there's two good intelligent people here, blah, blah, blah", and, hence, I think that helped me with passing the 11+ etc. etc.' That is, it may have given him confidence, and supportive teachers may have extrapolated other abilities from these tests and encouraged, credited, and marked his work positively. In any case, in 1971, when he was 11, he passed the 11+ examination, which was then required for access to grammar school. He treated this transition as something normal, so I asked him whether it was, or whether it was discussed at home, and he answered: 'And possibly was because it was – because I was male that I would go on to grammar school and then develop in a certain way.' He mentioned that neither his sister nor any of his half-brothers and sisters went on to higher education.

Passing the 11+ examination was a crucial, concrete enabling factor, although Berry did not stay in grammar school or take a linear path to higher education. However, he enjoyed grammar school, which I consider to have been an important experience for him, and which probably gave him a prospect on university, as grammar schools were meant to lead to university.

From 1971 to 1972, he attended grammar school in a county in eastern England that established a three, rather than a two, tier system of lower, middle, and upper schools, as recommended in the Plowden Report of 1967 (Education in England, 2014). He was given Latin and hymn books for assemblies, and each pupil received a Bible, but his school also organized so-called 'reversal days', when boys did girls' subjects and girls did boys' subjects, which was quite progressive. Berry enjoyed school:

> I felt at home. It was with people – as I said earlier – you – you turn up, and you get given a Bible, and you get [pause] – you – you can then have Latin lessons and Greek lessons, and, and you have assemblies, and it was kind of uniform. You turn up at grammar school, you have to wear a tie, jackets, and things [pause] and I kind of enjoyed it. As far as I can remember. And the things that they do, as I mentioned before, the gender role swapping day – it was great. Once every, you know, and I remember [hesitates] cross-country running. I remember playing rugby. I was part of the rugby team. Me, be in the rugby team? Oh, ok! [short laugh]. It was great!

In 1972, when Berry was 12 years old, his father and stepmother decided to leave the area. Berry did not recall all the reasons, but one was the violence of his mother's husband, who threatened the family. For a year, Berry went to a county middle school in East Anglia and later did O levels at an upper school until 1976. The educational system was different; because he lived in an area with a comprehensive system, Berry could not continue grammar school, and he missed it. He felt dragged off to a place he did not want to live and did not feel challenged at the middle and upper schools, and he switched off. The other pupils had not passed the 11+, and his teachers overlooked him. He felt bullied and picked on.

His father and stepmother were now running a pub, and the family lived in it. The atmosphere was not appropriate for children and teenagers, and it left no space for a family life. Instead, Berry was surrounded by adults and always had to help with the food, serve behind the bar, or play darts. Bikers, five football teams, and a women's darts team frequented the pub; it held discos twice a week and businessman's lunches; people played cribbage. Berry's father continued to be emotionally unstable and took it out on the children. Berry said, 'There was lots of kinds of violence at home, violence in the pub.' Later, he said: 'And I did have memories of living in the pub that really [pause] – my memories of that, not false memories of things that happened to me that I probably don't want to disclose [laughing while talking] at this point in time either.'

At 16, Berry left his family and school and moved to another city in the same county. He remembered:

> But my path – my paths were grammar school and that kind of education system. I would really liked to have gone through it, or the – what happened to me in terms of the split between under 16s and adults and working life on top of an educational life. You know. And actually have a family background, rather than one of work, and a stable family environment? Don't know what you mean. Because it has always been one of work or tied to the business of running a pub. Those sorts of things. [Pause] A decision leaving home – because violence is not really a decision, it's a reaction again. So you can [hesitates] – ok had enough of that.

From 1976 to 1982, Berry worked in catering as a chef, interrupted in 1978, when he was 18, by six months' backpacking in Central America. He interpreted it as a search, a spiritual journey to find himself or to find something he thought he had lost that was always with him.

In 1982, his mother contacted him and his sister and told them she wanted to meet, or at least to exchange letters. Berry started writing to her, and the correspondence went on for a year or two. Finally, his mother wanted to meet in a city where neither of them lived. When Berry got off the coach, he immediately recognized her, although he had not seen her for many years. They spent the day together, and in the evening he went back home.

In his spare time, Berry hung out at the student union and made friends with degree students. He found that he could speak their language, and they encouraged him to do his A levels. He stopped working and went to college for two years (1982–4) and, with funding, did his A levels in psychology, sociology, economics, and government policy. He passed all subjects.

He then moved to a large city and, while also working, became involved in the arts, a theatre group, and choreography. He visited his grandparents every other weekend. He took another trip, this time to Athens and Rhodes and then Crete, where he was invited to pick grapes in the mountains. A friend from home visited him, bringing university application forms; Berry filled them out, and his friend took them back. Here, social capital was crucial for Berry's educational upward mobility. From Greece, Berry travelled to Turkey and Israel, where he stayed on a kibbutz. He was travelling with friends around the Middle East when he received an invitation for an interview at a polytechnic university in England. He returned, and from 1989 to 1992, from 29 to 32 years old, Berry took a BA (Hons) in arts. His subjects were art history, contemporary art, mass media ideology, photography, English drama, and social anthropology, and he took an extra course in creative writing. He received a full grant and found his studies interesting. Toward the end, his grandparents were in need of care, and he visited every weekend until 1992, when they died. Finishing his undergraduate degree, Berry worked for about four years as a patient care technician, assisting patients in tasks they could not do for themselves, such as eating. A patient care technician takes orders from nurses.

In 2001, he was 41 years old and began part-time study for a Master's (MSc) degree in health policy with his fees paid.

It was two evenings a week for two years, which was interesting. And I really enjoyed that, because it was very academic-based. I think it was studying the processes of academia as well as contributing to it. ... Which is the epistemological approach to, if you like [hesitates] – how can you put it? [Pause] – the way that healthcare systems change in three countries [countries' names left out] with linkages to the OECD, the IMF, European Union, yeah, who are the, who are the drivers – which words are being used, who are the experts for those [pause] approaches that you would use to try and understand systematic change from a policy point of view.

Berry spoke most about his dissertation; Master's students in England are free to select the topic. He linked his Master's study to his precarious experiences as a child:

> Plus, I – throughout this whole kind of period of those kind of emotional traumas, at two-and-a-half, I didn't used to speak very often. Words just – er, well, what are words? Which like [incomprehensible] throughout a life of them, you are doing a Master's [incomprehensible] epistemologically, epistemological power of the word, and just kind of go 'I know exactly what you mean,' you know? Because the word, I rarely [pause], you know, it's one thing I do remember, is my lack of speech. And maybe I could be analyzed by an educational psychologist or this kind of stuff, which is possibly why I like working in the environment where I'm working in alongside psychologists and health people because I find answers to questions I still have.

This section of the interview might be regarded as the culmination. Berry stated how closely his studies were tied to coping with his childhood experiences. Studying enabled him to seek and to find words for clear descriptions and analysis, replacing the speechlessness resulting from emotional and social insecurity. Higher education afforded Berry the opportunity to seek truth and gain orientation, which comforted him.

About six years after finishing his degree, Berry considered pursuing a PhD and was offered places, but in 2012 he was 52 years old, had not decided what he would do with a PhD, and he had no funding. Again, without material support, educational upward mobility is rarely possible, which prevents people like him from earning the highest educational credentials.

Berry laid the ground for the new by leaving his father's family at the age of 16. By escaping its violent chaos, he left a social context that was smothering him. While working, he was open to more experiences and hung out with university students, who encouraged him to do his A levels. Later, still working, he moved in with university students. In a way, his social milieu was never homogeneous, first living with his unskilled working-class parents, then with his paternal grandparents as rural gentry, later with his father and step-mother and (half)sibling(s), and, for a short time, his mother and her violent husband. The dominant experiences of his childhood and youth were precariousness, violence, danger, and anxiety, but he had some years of quite stable social circumstances in the loving and safe environment provided by his grandparents. They might have built a social foundation for openness and seeking new experiences. In terms of social change, in leaving his milieu to live and travel inde-pendently, he realized a huge change. On the other hand, he stuck to his milieu by acquiring higher education step by step, starting at the polytechnic, completing the part-time Master's program, and considering a PhD, while working professionally in health and social services.

4.8.1.3   Overcoming neglect by finding oneself in higher education

We discussed Karin Eichner's educational upward mobility in rela-tion to institutional support, the study authorization examination, but her story is more complex. She was born in 1972 in a small town in upper Austria. Her mother was 27 years old and from Transylvania. When she was about one and a half years old, her own mother died, and, as soon as she could, she had to run the household for her father and three brothers. She would have loved to become a hairdresser – she even went to a shop and asked for an apprenticeship – but her father forbade it and told her to work at home. After the end of her compulsory education, she worked in a factory, as a cleaner, and in a retail shop as a packer, which was the only job she enjoyed. At home, she watched a lot of TV.

When Eichner was born, her father was 34, the youngest of 13 siblings from rural Austria, and the only one who migrated to the city. An alcoholic, he worked as a taxi driver. Eichner never knew when he would come home, how drunk or aggressive or sad he might be, or whether he would come home at all. She lived with immense insecu-rity and unreliability. He beat her and her older sister, but she did not even think about telling anyone. She tried to stay away as much as possible. She was allowed to play outside with neighborhood kids in the courtyard of the block of flats, but she never invited them in.

She started kindergarten at the age of four and was looking forward to it very much. Her sister hated school, always struggled, and, since

Eichner saw herself as her sister's opposite, she assumed that she would enjoy it:

> And I was absolutely happy in elementary school, so that was fun, and I learnt very very easily. I found nothing difficult, learnt by heart everything quickly and had talent in the written area, German, foreign languages, although this was not yet an issue in elementary school, but it was something exceptional, that somebody came along who enjoyed school. My parents didn't expect it [laughs]. So, after holidays, I always was very much looking forward to being able to go to school because it was simply fascinating to me, so, I simply wanted to know everything, about life, about geography, history, everything, yes.

Eichner performed very well. She recalled an incident with her father that had a big impact on her:

> And my father, whom I loved very much, although he was very difficult, said once, yes – one wants recognition as a child, and when one is good at school, and no recognition is ever mentioned, and once there was this sentence: '[Karin] is so smart, she has to go to university.' Yes, this is a sentence that stayed with me for a long time, yes, although I didn't know then what it meant, university, but my father had an image of professionals – they live better than him – there were no specific deliberations because he knew nothing about it – you see, in our family, there are no professionals – but he thought, the professionals are better off, and he somehow wanted that for me. Yes, that was something quite exceptional too, that he mentioned it.

The last sentence shows the neglect she suffered: being noticed and wished well were rare events in her childhood. Later in the interview, she returned to the point:

> I mean, this sentence was mentioned perhaps twice, yes. But this [10-second pause], yes, this just meant something to me. There was a plan for me, or there was some thought for me that might fit, and I heard a pride resonating, and yes. While studying, I often had the feeling, I am doing this for my father, too, although for a

long time now he no longer knows it, but I know for certain that he would be proud somehow, and that was a reason too, yes.

Eichner felt closer to her father than to her mother, perhaps because of this sentence in which he recognized her abilities and wished her well. In contrast, her mother never said anything about her daughter's abilities and made no effort to develop a vision of her daughter's future life.

She also denied her the chance to go to an upper secondary general school. At the end of elementary school, Eichner's class teacher and even the headmistress tried to persuade her mother to allow her to go to the *Gymnasium*, but her mother decided against it, arguing that there was no sense to it.

'No, you don't need to do this.' You see? In doing so, my mother never – so my mother had no plan at all for me. Some mothers say, 'You will marry and have children', but for me, there was simply no plan, not even that one. So there was no plan, you see, and there was – well, so I was not asked whether I wanted this, she simply – you know, it is not necessary, or you don't need to do this, so no, you are not allowed. It was just not seen as necessary.

Eichner expressed great bitterness about her mother's action in the interview; she felt completely neglected by her mother. When I asked about her father's participation in this decision, she said there was none, but she did not call it neglect.

At *Hauptschule*, Eichner was bored. For four years, she was the best pupil in the class. She liked meeting friends at school and an English teacher: 'Well, she praised us a lot, and she was – she actually, for all we did well – she was an older woman who was very, very, very motherly and incredibly smart, and she did it playfully. She prepared lessons brilliantly, and she was simply fond of us all. She was a teacher, heart and soul, yes. This was a good one.' Eichner did not mention any other teachers she appreciated.

When she was about 11 or 12 years old, she began to explore the local library: 'That was the great realization – so there is a place where you don't have to pay – because money was always an issue – there are books that you can take home, and that was a sensation for me. From that time onward, I have always read books.' The library fed Eichner's hunger to learn about the world and probably allowed her to escape her real world. About this time, her sister was beaten a lot and went to school distraught. A teacher became aware and had several conversations with the parents, and, from then onward, they went to parents' evenings regularly.

In her final year of *Hauptschule*, Eichner's headmaster, who was also a career counsellor, advised her to go to the *Handelsakademie*, an upper secondary vocational school that also offered the highest school-leaving certificate. Her marks were too good to finish her compulsory schooling with the Poly, a one-year school that aims to direct pupils with the lowest school-leaving degrees toward vocational education and apprenticeships. The headmaster did not suggest *Gymnasium*, although both schools, *Handelsakademie* and *Gymnasium*, were in the same building. Eichner asked him whether there was a school where she could draw, but he said there was not. She believed he meant to give the most practical answer, advising her to go to an upper vocational school that prepared girls for office work.

Only one of her classmates went on to the *Handelsakademie* with her; all the others went to the Poly. Eichner did not miss them, but at the *Handelsakademie* she was deeply bored by the subjects: accounting, costing, even subjects she had formerly enjoyed, such as German and English. The situation at home grew worse. At 14, Eichner became aggressive and started to resist her mother. Her sister moved out without any improvement. When Eichner was 15, her father had a car accident, lapsed into a coma, and died. Her mother was in financial trouble and said she could not support her daughter financially for the five years of *Handelsakademie*; she should do an apprenticeship to earn her own salary. At that time, finding an apprenticeship as an office clerk was easy, especially coming from the *Handelsakademie*, so Eichner dropped out, despite wanting to continue, however dissatisfied, and started a three-year apprenticeship as an office clerk.

She struggled, demanding to learn something. After her first year, she was already managing her own task areas, such as purchasing and selling, and received a lot of praise. She graduated from the parallel vocational school with distinction. During this time, her wish to study became more concrete and helped her to bear the remaining three years:

Yes, and at the end of the apprenticeship, we knew there was something like the *Studienberechtigungsprüfung* [study authorization examination], so in the back of your mind, there was always university, and so, I don't know, I got this somewhere, somewhere I, somewhere I read this, that that there exists something like a *Studienberechtigungsprüfung*, and I inquired, and yes, I knew I was going to do that. I did not yet know what I wanted to study, so I didn't have a professional goal but the calling to study.

The *Studienberechtigungsprüfung* was among the few alternative routes to higher education, as discussed in Section 4.7.3, and it was crucial for Eichner's educational upward mobility. She had to select her study subject, social sciences, and pass examinations in six subjects: German, maths, English, history, geography, and social sciences. To become eligible for a study grant, she knew she had to work for four years, and following her apprenticeship, working on as an office clerk, she enrolled in courses to prepare for the maths and English examinations. She enjoyed learning and did not find it very difficult. For the other subjects, she sought out learning materials at the university and studied on her own in the evenings. In the last month of her compulsory four years of employment, she passed her final study authorization examination.

First, she enrolled in socioeconomics and felt: 'Yes and that brought up with it a lot of joy and a great deal of pride – to hold my student ID card in my hand and – Wow, I have this – I am able to study, ah, this I have prepared on my own for myself, and this pleasant anticipation of learning, so this was all very strongly there, and, at the same time, of course, incredible anxieties emerged.'

Shortly thereafter, she attended a sociology lecture and changed her study subject: 'I was sitting there, and my mouth was hanging open, and after an hour, I thought, wow, now time has passed so quickly, something I hadn't experienced in the other subjects, and I – yes, it just interested me completely. It was exciting. I thought: I can study this, yes, this is about people, about society, a bit about history and that's it, yes.'

In another interview sequence, Eichner described the aha-experience in this lecture and repeated that this subject was exactly what she was interested in. She described herself as a very disciplined student, well-prepared months before the examinations, in contrast to other students who started to study only a week or two before. She attributed her good habits to her working experience and saw it as an advantage. Lehmann (2008) describes similar interpretations of work experience among first-generation students at a Canadian university. In addition to the subject content, she found an encouraging professor from a working-class background, and she built many deep friendships among her fellow students, still in place at the time of the interview, and providing a lot of self-affirmation.

> I felt great. That was a very, very good time. That was the time when an incredible amount happened in my private life, when I began to leave my childhood story behind. I mean, this, of course, you can't completely, but then it was not as present, and it did not determine my life so much, and I dealt with it a lot, a lot, a lot, a lot, and yes. And I felt increasingly better, so I could sense myself, my own life, and – good.

The essence of her study time: 'the best time in my life until now'.

After obtaining her Master's degree, she worked freelance on a research project and started to plan a PhD, but the project stopped for six months, and Eichner had to teach at a further education institution. She hated it and applied for work at several companies, landing a job with a start-up firm as executive director. She left after two years because her workload was so small. She went back to the further education institution and offered courses for unemployed people, while also taking courses in drawing therapy and computers. She had become tired of being 'the motivator and the superior'. A colleague informed her about a new post in a different organization, and she was still employed in its education department at the time of the interview.

In Eichner's life history, an abundance of factors were crucial for her educational upward mobility; very good marks, an alternative route to university in the form of the study authorization examination, and grant support were material factors making study possible for her. However, the outstanding feature in her history is the meaning higher education had for her, as a place where, for the first time, she felt she was herself and could leave her experiences of neglect behind. Being yourself is feeling secure.

Two new elements were crucial for her upward mobility and, thus, social change. First, she relied on herself a lot as a result of her social circumstances. Her parents worked outside the home, and her father often did not come home. She had to do for herself, and, moreover, she kept much of her distress to herself. This containment was the starting point for her search, which also required a certain openness. In contrast to her sister, who was beaten up more often, Eichner was not broken, and she was allowed to play outside, which gave her a certain leeway to discover new things, such as the library.

The other line of the new came from her father, who already differed from his siblings. He opened possibilities with his vision: '[Karin] is smart, she will study someday.' He gave her a drop of self-confidence and a history of departure to start something new. She was not completely tied to her family and milieu. The neglect left her room. Since she experienced her family as terrible, her search pointed away from them. Something new was possible, but she had to deploy enormous effort. In higher education, she found her essence and left her experiences of abuse and neglect behind.

Note that patterns of emotional precariousness are not exclusive to a certain social context or milieu or even class. Berry, Mutz, and Eichner came from very different social contexts within what I frame as working class. Berry's background was Methodist English rural gentry, as embodied by his grandparents, with whom he stayed for five years in his childhood, but his parents were unskilled workers. Mutz was also from a rural area, but his people were poor and commercially dependent, and he was strongly influenced by his uncle's social-democratic orientation. Eichner's milieu was also unskilled working class but more urban, probably less religious, and it offered more educational resources, such as the library. These varying circumstances in which precariousness was experienced could be adduced as evidence of the importance of individual character over social context for educational upward mobility. However, in each of these three examples, social structures were clearly decisive. To address the importance of mentality, or mindset, I will now examine how a sense of knowing the truth can provide security and/or comfort beyond these three life histories.

4.8.2   Excursus: the relation of truth to security and/or comfort

In all three life histories analyzed above, higher education was a place where abandoned, deeply shaken, violated, and neglected people found ways to gain security through calculation, orientation, and sense of self. Here, I want to explore truth *as a dimension of education* that provides security and comfort. In precarious situations, security is the first aim, and comfort perhaps second, when security cannot be reached. I will set out five ways that truth can lead to security and comfort, starting with the most tangible. My point is that understanding mental processes can enable us to design our educational institutions to support healing and growth; we have choices and can teach and conduct research in a way that aspires to discover truth, not merely to raise funds, for example. Providing students with the tools to develop their own interests and questions and to seek answers is a sociopolitical act that especially benefits students from precarious backgrounds.

The relations of truth to security and comfort are:

1. To know something provides security, defined as orientation, order, firmness, reliability, a foundation (see Young, 2007, on 'powerful knowledge'). These qualities are in sharp contrast to the chaos at home: unreliable parents, absent or neglectful parents, abusive parents. The search for truth takes place in lecture halls, libraries, archives, at quiet desks and in laboratories, places that are clean, orderly, radiating a positive atmosphere, in contrast to the dirty, ugly, noisy, violent locations in which some children are imprisoned. The more learning locations are designed to seek truth, the less their occupants' origin and social, economic, and cultural background matters. In fact, most of our lecture halls, universities, libraries, and archives are still culturally linked to middle- and upper-class cultural and economic backgrounds. Remember that Johnson was overwhelmed by a bathroom at Oxford. However, referencing Bourdieu and Passeron (1977), once working-class people expend the huge effort to make it to these places, once they know the rules – how to use a library or an archive; how to pose a question in a lecture or to follow a laboratory protocol – a whole world opens to them. According to the Habermasian ideal of communication without hierarchies, the fewer hierarchies created and practiced, the fewer impediments to seeking truth. Thus, the less professors and lecturers are interested in their positions, and the more they are interested in conveying their subject content, the more likely it is that social, economic, and cultural 'strangers' will pose a question and participate in a mutually enriching discussion. At good locations for the pursuit

of truth, participants know they will not be slapped or ridiculed; that others will behave in a certain, respectful way; and that space will be provided for calming down, concentrating, and coming to oneself.

2. Sometimes, seeking truth does not mean achieving truth; no clear or fixed answers are possible. Still, the process itself can create security in going deeper, discarding superficial assumptions, knowing how to detect unsatisfactory answers. Security consists in achieving a comprehensive knowledge that builds a foundation for apt questions.

3. Intellectual activity, deliberation, saturation in ideas that cannot be realized otherwise, mentally, corporally, emotionally, may not achieve the security of truth but are a secure methodology or a methodology of securing. Here, cognitive understanding, memorizing, writing can help to capture something, to keep it in mind, and to prevent it from dissolving and disappearing.

4. Seeking truth can also provide comfort. Here, understanding means *grasping* something; it is accessible, not detached. We are not alone, not separated from it, but hold it in our minds, and the connection can be comforting.

5. Seeking truth and reaching an understanding of something sad, such as precarious childhood experiences, can provide meaning, not in the sense of a destination or fate, but in tracing something that still exists. We cannot change the past, but we may learn that it was not our fault; we did not miss an opportunity to remove it from the world or to change it for the better. The knowledge that we could not have done anything is calming, comforting, and provides peace.

Finally, I want to mention Habermas's idea of the relationship of knowledge to human interest because it indicates why educational institutions should be designed to enable the search for truth, not simply a money-making career: 'In self-reflection knowledge for the sake of knowledge attains congruence with the interest in autonomy and responsibility. The emancipatory cognitive interest aims at the pursuit of reflection as such.... in the power of self-reflection, knowledge and interest are one' (1971, p. 314). Habermas argues from an anthropological perspective that the structure of language bestows autonomy and responsibility on its users. Thus, autonomy and responsibility are universal and independent of culture. I have posited that seeking knowledge is a universal human need, but it is nevertheless much more important and urgent for people from socially and emotionally precarious backgrounds, as others can more easily mistake easygoing life contexts for autonomy and responsibility. Habermas's fundamental anthropological perspective can be related to different social, mental, cultural, and economic contexts, and I would argue for the importance of offering people from socially precarious backgrounds educational institutions that are as free from hierarchy as possible in their time and place – institutions whose sole purpose is truth-seeking.

5
Summary and Conclusions

This study on working-class educational upward mobility is part of the research field of social inequality in education. While most studies in the field focus on discrimination, barriers, and difficulties working-class people face in education, this study explores the contexts and circumstances that enable their success. The life histories of educationally successful people from working-class families brought to light all sorts of discrimination, barriers, and difficulties but also ways of overcoming them and, more to the point, social contexts favorable for working-class people. The study, therefore, connects to the research field on social mobility and other studies on working-class educational upward mobility.

The literature review revealed that most studies explaining educational upward mobility focus on *one* dimension: for example, an individual's motives and aspirations. My study demonstrated how several circumstances and factors *interrelate* and *together* enable the educational upward mobility of working-class people. In fact, in all the interviewees' life histories, more than one factor was crucial. For example, I demonstrated how the development of individual aspirations to participate in higher education was embedded in family histories and parents' secure employment conditions, which provided a certain level of income. Furthermore, few studies on enabling circumstances have been based on empirical data; the present analysis of 18 life histories of educationally upwardly mobile people from working-class families starts to fill this gap.

For my analysis of the exceptional educational upward mobility of people from working-class families, I chose the theoretical framework of Bourdieu and some of Rosenthal's methodology. This approach implies several new steps. First, so far, most have used Bourdieu's framework to analyze barriers to working-class people's education. In contrast, I demonstrated how his concept of habitus can be used to analyze processes of change, as educational upward mobility among working-class people means a change of social milieu, sense of belonging, and class. Thus, my study also demonstrates that the concept of habitus is *not* deterministic and that criticism, mainly in the English-language literature, on this point is wrong and shows a misunderstanding of Bourdieu's concept of habitus.

Second, I use the parts of Rosenthal's methodology that ensure fine-grained, objective analysis but shifted from creating types to detecting social contexts and circumstances that are crucial for educational upward mobility. Third, this departure enabled me to link Bourdieu's theory with Rosenthal's method to reveal the complex scenarios that can lead to educational upward mobility.

The enabling circumstances and conditions identified are:

- parents' secure employment and material conditions, enabling the development of aspirations and supportive, education-affirming socialization;
- changes in objective structures, of which changes of policy that improved the economic situation for the working classes and changes in cultural values are the most important;
- lack of actualization of habitus, forcing people toward new aims and directions in life, one of which can be education;
- processes of becoming conscious of social hierarchies and one's situation in society, which could be improved by obtaining a university degree;
- pedagogical efforts by educational staff that help working-class children to succeed in education;
- gender in relation to hierarchies that help men and special educational policies that help women; and
- educational institutions that support alternative routes, apart from the mainstream acquisition of A levels or *Matura*, to higher education.

Bourdieu mentions most of these circumstances and conditions but without systematic analysis, another gap my study starts to fill.

Analysis of the empirical data led to a new realization of the importance and strength of a complex mental dimension for educational upward mobility. Several interviewees from precarious social backgrounds sought truth in higher education, which provided security and/or comfort. For them, going to university was a way to overcome existentially threatening childhood experiences. I was able to detect these facilitators because Bourdieu's concept of habitus includes perceptions, attitudes, logic, and emotions but not this mental dimension, which contributes to a deeper, more comprehensive conceptualization of habitus and suggests a new design strategy for more effective higher education institutions and practices.

To enable working-class people to seek truth, educational institutions should be nonhierarchical, offering the means to develop and to pursue questions, and going beyond the aim of employability. These guidelines are decisive for educational reforms aiming for greater social equality.

As a comparative study, findings suggest no *fundamental* differences in paths toward educational upward mobility between Austria and England. Surprisingly, given their different labor market structures; welfare state regimes; and educational systems, institutions, and policies, the conditions crucial for educational upward mobility are generally similar: for example, massive changes to cultural, social, and living conditions for women as part of an overall process of modernization. A second conclusion that can be drawn from the lack of larger differences between the two countries is that educational upward mobility requires such basic conditions as education-affirmative socialization and the search for truth, which are not bound to one society or country.

Finally, my study can be read as a special account on *a certain period in the process of social change* by demonstrating how structural changes in economy, policy, gender relations, and culture changed parents' views, perspectives, and attitudes that affected changes in child-rearing at home and in schools, leading to the development of new conditions that enabled the children to seek higher education, to change class, and to conduct lifestyles different from those of their parents.

Bibliography

Absolventenverband (n.d.). *50 Jahre ehrenamtliche Arbeit für den Zweiten Bildungsweg 1961–2011*. Linz: Trauner Druck.

Albrecht-Heide, A. (1972). *Bildungsaufstieg durch Deformation. Studenten des zweitenBildungsweges vom Braunschweig-Kolleg.* Teil I. Hamburg: Stiftung Europa-Kolleg Hamburg, Fundament-Verlag Dr. Sasse & Co.

Alheit, P., Rheinländer, K., & Watermann, R. (2008). Zwischen Bildungsaufstieg und Karriere: Studienperspektiven nicht-traditioneller Studierender. *Zeitschrift für Erziehungswissenschaft, 11*, 577–606.

Arbeiterkammer Wien (2013). *Nachhilfe in Österreich. Bundesweite Elternbefragung 2013.* Retrieved December 12, 2013, from http://www.ifes. at/sites/default/files/downloads/nachhilfe_in_oesterreich_2013.pdf.

Ball, S.J. (2003). *Class strategies and the education market. The middle class and social advantage.* London: RoutledgeFalmer.

Ball, S.J. (2006). *Education policy and social class: the selected works of Stephen Ball.* Oxon, New York: Routledge.

Ball, S.J., Bowe, R., & Gerwitz, S. (1997). Circuits of schooling. A sociological exploration of parental choice of school in social-class contexts. In A.H. Halsey, H. Lauder, P. Brown, & A.S. Wells (Eds.), *Education, culture, economy and society* (pp. 409–21). Oxford: Oxford University Press.

Ball, S.J., Davies, J., David, M., & Reay, D. (2002). 'Classification' and 'judgement': Social class and the 'cognitive structures' of choice of higher education. *British Journal of Sociology of Education, 23*, 51–72.

Becker, R. (2007). Wie nachhaltig sind die Bildungsaufstiege wirklich? Eine Realanalyse der Studie von Fuchs und Sixt (2007) über die soziale Vererbung von Bildungserfolgen in der Generationenabfolge. *Kölner Zeitschrift für Soziologie und Sozialpsychologie, 59* (3), 512–523.

Becker, R., & Hecken, A. (2008). Warum werden Arbeiterkinder vom Studium an Universitaeten abgelenkt? Eine empirische Ueberpruefung der 'Ablenkungsthese' von Mueller und Pollak (2007) und ihre Erweiterung durch Hillmert und Jacob (2003). *Kölner Zeitschrift für Soziologie und Sozialpsychologie, 60*, 3–29.

Becker, R., & Hecken, A.E. (2009a). Higher education or vocational education? An empirical test of the rational action model of educational choices suggested by Breen and Goldthorpe (1997) and Esser (1999). *Acta Sociologica, 52* (1), 25–45.

Becker, R., & Hecken, A.E. (2009b). Why are working-class children diverted from universities? *European Sociological Review, 25* (2), 233–50.

Berger, P.L., & Kahlert, H. (Eds.) (2005). *Institutionalisierte Ungleichheiten. Wie das Bildungssystem Chancen blockiert*, Weinheim: Juventa.

Blau, P.M., & Duncan, O.D. (1967). *The American occupational structure*, New York: John Wiley & Sons, Inc.

Blossfeld, H.-P.& Shavit, Y. (1993). Dauerhafte Ungleichheiten – Zur Veränderung des Einflusses der sozialen Herkunft auf die Bildungschancen in dreizehn industrialisierten Ländern, *Zeitschrift für Pädagogik*, 39, 25–52.

Bohnsack, R. (2003). Dokumentarische Methode. In R. Bohnsack, W. Marotzki, & M. Meuser (Eds.) *Hauptbegriffe Qualitative Sozialforschung. Ein Wörterbuch* (pp. 40–4). Opladen: Leske+Budrich.

Bohnsack, R. (2007). Dokumentarische Methode und praxeologische Wissenssoziologie. In R. Schützeichel (Ed.), *Handbuch Wissenssoziologie und Wissensforschung* (pp. 180–90). Konstanz: UKV.

Boudon, R. (1974). *Education, opportunity and social inequality: Changing prospects in western society.* New York: John Wiley & Sons.

Bourdieu, P. (1983). Der Habitus als Vermittlung zwischen Struktur und Praxis. In *Zur Soziologie der symbolischen Formen* (pp. 125–58). Frankfurt am Main: Suhrkamp. (Reprinted from Postface à E. Panófsky. *Architecture gothique et pensée scolastique*, pp. 133–67. Paris, Éd. de Minuit, 1967).

Bourdieu, P. (1990). Structures, habitus, practices. In *The logic of practice* (pp. 52–65). Cambridge, UK: Polity Press.

Bourdieu, P. (1998). *Practical reason: On the theory of action.* Stanford: Stanford University Press.

Bourdieu, P. (2000). *Pascalian meditations.* Stanford: Stanford University Press.

Bourdieu, P. (2005). Habitus. In J. Hillier & E. Rooksby (Eds.) *Habitus: A sense of place*, 2nd Ed. (pp. 43–9). Farnham, UK: Ashgate.

Boudieu, P. (2009), Struktur, Habitus, Praxis. In *Entwurf einer Theorie der Praxis auf der ethnologischen Grundlage der kabylischen Gesellschaft* (pp. 139–203). Frankfurt am Main: Suhrkamp.

Bourdieu, P., & Boltanski, L. (1977). Formal qualifications and occupational hierarchies: The relationship between the production system and the reproduction system. *Reorganizing Education*, Sage Annual Review of Social and Educational Change, *1*, 61–9.

Bourdieu, P., Chamboredon, J.-C., & Passeron, J.-C. (1991). *The craft of sociology.Epistemological preliminaries*, Ed. B. Krais, trans. R. Nice. Berlin and New York: Walter de Gruyter.

Bourdieu, P., & Passeron, J.-C. (1971). *Die Illusion der Chancengleichheit. Untersuchungen zur Soziologie des Bildungswesens am Beispiel Frankreichs.* Stuttgart: Klett Verlag.

Bourdieu, P., & Passeron, J.-C. (1977). *Reproduction in education, society and culture.* London: Sage.

Bourdieu, P., & Passeron, J.-C. (1979). *The inheritors. French students and their relation to culture.* Chicago: University of Chicago Press.

Bourdieu, P., Passeron, J.-C., & de Saint Martin, M. (1994). *Academic discourse: Linguistic misunderstanding and professional power.* Cambridge, UK: Polity Press.

Bourdieu, P., & Wacquant, L.J.D. (1992). The Purpose of Reflexive Sociology (The Chicago Workshop), in *An Invitation to Reflexive Sociology* (pp. 60–215). Cambridge: Polity Press.

Bowl, M. (2003). *Non-traditional entrants in higher education: they talk about people like me.* Stoke on Trent: Trentham.

Breen, R., & Goldthorpe, J.H. (1997). Explaining educational differentials: Towards a formal rational action theory. *Rationality and Society, 9* (3), 275–305.

Breen, R., & Jonsson, J. (2005). Inequality of opportunity in comparative perspective: Recent research on educational attainment and social mobility. *Annual Review of Sociology, 31,* 223–43.

Breen, R., & Jonsson, J. (2007). Explaining change in social fluidity: Educational equalization and educational expansion in twentieth-century Sweden. *American Journal of Sociology, 112* (6), 1775–810.

Breen, R., & Luijkx, R. (2004). Conclusions. In R. Breen (Ed.) *Social Mobility in Europe* (pp. 383–410). Oxford: Oxford University Press.

Brendel, S. (1998). *Arbeitertöchter beißen sich durch. Bildungsbiographien und Sozialisationsbedingungen junger Frauen aus der Arbeiterschicht.* Weinheim and München: Juventa.

Briar, C. (1997). *Working for women? Gendered work and welfare policies in twentieth-century Britain.* London: UCL Press.

Bublitz, H. (1980). *Ich gehörte irgendwie so nirgends hin ... Arbeitertöchter an Hochschulen.* Giessen: Focus Verlag.

Burke, P.J. (2002). *Accessing education: effectively widening participation.* Stoke on Trent: Trentham.

Butschek, F. (1985). *Die österreichische Wirtschaft im 20. Jahrhundert.* Wien: Österreichisches Institut für Wirtschaftsforschung.

Central Statistical Office (1986). *Social Trends 16. 1986 Edition.* London: Her Majesty's Stationery Office.

Central Statistical Office (1987). *Social Trends 17. 1987 Edition.* London: Her Majesty's Stationery Office.

Chamberlayne, P., Bornat, J., & Apitzsch, U. (Eds.) (2004). *Biographical methods and professional practice: An international perspective.* Bristol: Polity Press.

Chamberlayne, P., Bornat, J., & Wengraf, T. (Eds.) (2000). *The turn to biographical methods in social science: Comparative issues and examples.* London: Routledge.

Chamberlayne, P., & King, A. (1996). Biographical approaches in comparative work: The 'cultures of care' project. In L. Hantrais, & S. Mangen (Eds.) *Cross-national research methods in the social sciences* (pp. 95–104). London: Pinger.

Chamberlayne, P., & King, A. (2000). *Cultures of care. Biographies of carers in Britain and the two Germanies.* Bristol: Policy Press.

Chamberlayne, P., Rustin, M., & Wengraf, T. (Eds.) (2002). *Biography and social exclusion in Europe: Experiences and life journeys.* Bristol: Policy Press.

Chitty, C. (2009). *Education policy in Britain,* 2nd Ed. Basingstoke: Palgrave Macmillan.

Christopher, R. (2009). *A carpenter's daughter: A working-class woman in higher education.* Rotterdam: Sense Publishers.

Clancy, K. (1997). Academic as anarchist: Working-class lives into middle-class culture. In P. Mahony, & C. Zmroczek (Eds.) *Class matters: 'Working-class' women's perspectives on social class* (pp. 44–52). London: Taylor & Francis.

Collins, R. (1979). *The Credential Society. An Historical Sociology of Education and Stratification.* New York: Academic Press.

Coxon, A.P.M., & Jones, C.L. (Eds.) (1975). *Social mobility.* Harmondsworth: Penguin.

Crompton, R. (2008). *Class and Stratification,* 3rd Ed. Cambridge, UK: Polity Press.

Dean, J., Bradley, K., Choppin, B., &Vincent, D. (1979). *The sixth form and its alternatives.*Windsor: NFER Publishing Company.

Department of Employment (1977). *New Earnings Survey 1977. Part A: Report and key results.* London: Government Statistical Service.

Education in England (2014). *The Plowden Report (1967). Children and their primary schools. A Report for the Central Advisory Council (England).* London: Her Majesty's Stationery Office 1967. Retrieved March 10, 2014, from http://www.educationengland.org.uk/documents/plowden/.

Erikson, R., & Goldthorpe, J.H. (1992). *The constant flux. A study of class mobility in industrial societies.* Oxford: Clarendon Press.

Erikson, R., & Jonsson, J. (1996). *Can education be equalized? The Swedish case in comparative perspective.* Boulder: Westview Press.

Ermisch, J. (1989). Divorce: Economic antecedents and aftermath. In H. Joshi (Ed.), *The changing population of Britain* (pp. 42–55). Oxford: Basil Blackwell.

Esping-Andersen, G. (1990). *The three worlds of welfare capitalism.* Cambridge, UK: Polity Press.

Francis, J.C. (1976). *The social organisation, culture and function of a sixth form college: Student and staff perceptions.* Unpublished doctoral dissertation, University of Southampton.

Frankl, K.H. (1996). Die katholische Kirche in Österreich von 1945 bis 1995—die Geschichte einer Erschöpfung? In F. Csoklich, M. Opis, E. Petrik, & H. Schnuderl (Eds.) *ReVisionen. Katholische Kirche in der Zweiten Republik* (pp. 17–40). Graz, Wien, and Köln: Verlag Styria.

Fuchs, M., & Sixt, M. (2007a). Replik auf den Diskussionsbeitrag von Rolf Becker. Bildungsmobilität über drei Generationen. Was genau bewirken Bildungsaufstiege für die Kinder der Aufsteiger? *Kölner Zeitschrift für Soziologie und Sozialpsychologie, 59* (3), 534–5.

Fuchs, M., & Sixt, M. (2007b). Zur Nachhaltigkeit von Bildungsaufstiegen. Soziale Vererbung von Bildungserfolgen über mehrere Generationen. *Kölner Zeitschrift für Soziologie und Sozialpsychologie, 59* (1), 1–29.

Gandara, P. (1995). *Over the ivy walls: The educational mobility of low-income Chicanos.* Albany: State University of New York Press.

Gemmeke, J. (1983). *Die Englische Open University. Eine Studie über Entstehungsbedingungen, Verlauf und Folgen einer bildungspolitischen Reform.* Frankfurt am Main and Bern, Peter Lang.

Gillard, D. (2011). *Education in England: A brief history.* Retrieved January 8, 2014, from http://www.educationengland.org.uk/history.

Goldman, R. (Ed.) (2012 [1968]). *Breakthrough: Autobiographical accounts of the education of some socially disadvantaged children.* Oxon and New York: Routledge.

Goldthorpe, J.H. (1985). Soziale Mobilität und Klassenbildung. Zur Erneuerung einer Tradition soziologischer Forschung. In H. Strasser, & J.H. Goldthorpe (Eds.) *Die Analyse sozialer Ungleichheit* (pp. 174–204). Opladen: Westdeutscher Verlag.

Goldthorpe, J.H. (1987). The experience of social mobility. In *Social Mobility and Class Structure in Modern Britain*, 2nd Ed. (pp. 217–301). Oxford: Clarendon Press.

Goldthorpe, J.H. (1996). Class analysis and the reorientation of class theory: The case of persisting differentials in educational attainment. *British Journal of Sociology, 47* (3), 481–505.

Goldthorpe, J.H., & Lockwood, D. (1963). Affluence and the British class structure. *Sociological Review, 11* (2), 133–63.

Goldthorpe, J.H., Payne, C., & Llewelley, C. (1978). Trends in class mobility. *Sociology, 12* (3), 441–68.

Goodwin, L.L. (2002). *Resilient spirits: Disadvantaged students making it at an elite university.* New York: RoutledgeFalmer.

Goodwin, L.L. (2006). *Graduating class: Disadvantaged students crossing the bridge of higher education.* Albany: State University New York Press.

Grenfell, M. (2004). *Pierre Bourdieu: Agent provocateur.* London and New York: Continuum.

Groß, M. (2008). *Klassen, Schichten, Mobilität. Eine Einführung.* Wiesbaden: Verlag für Sozialwissenschaften.

Grüner, G. (1980). *Alternative zum Gymnasium: Die berufsbildenden höheren Schulen Österreichs.* Weinheim: Beltz.

Haas, H. (2000). Der 'Anschluß'. In E. Tálos, E. Hanisch, W. Neugebauer, & R. Sieder (Eds.) *NS-Herrschaft in Österreich, Ein Handbuch* (pp. 26–54). Wien: öbv.

Habermas, J. (1971). Knowledge and human interests: A general perspective. In *Knowledge and human interest* (pp. 301–17). Boston: Beacon Press.

Hall, P., & Soskice, D. (Eds.) (2001). *Varieties of capitalism: Institutional foundations of comparative advantage.* New York: Oxford University Press.

Haller, M. (1989). *Klassenstrukturen und Mobilität in fortgeschrittenen Gesellschaften. Eine vergleichende Analyse der Bundesrepublik Deutschland, Österreichs, Frankreichs und der Vereinigten Staaten von Amerika.* Frankfurt and New York: Campus.

Halsey, A.H. (1987). Social trends since World War II. In Central Statistical Office (pp. 11–19). London: Her Majesty's Stationery Office.

Hanisch, E. (1994). *Der Lange Schatten des Staates. Österreichische Gesellschaftsgeschichte im 20. Jahrhundert.* Wien: Ueberreuter.

Harker, R., Mahar, C., & Wilkes, C. (1990). *An introduction to the work of Pierre Bourdieu. The practice of theory.* Houndmills, Basingstoke: Macmillan Press.

Harnoncourt, P. (1996). Von der Liturgischen Bewegung zur Liturgierform des Zweiten Vatikanums. In F. Csoklich, M. Opis, E. Petrik, & H. Schnuderl (Eds.), *ReVisionen. Katholische Kirche in der Zweiten Republik* (pp. 197–201). Graz, Wien, and Köln: Styria.

Harper, S.R., & Griffin, K.A. (2011). Opportunity beyond affirmative action: How low-income and working-class black male achievers access highly selective, high-cost colleges and universities. *Harvard Journal of African American Policy*. Retrieved April 23, 2013, from http://isites.harvard.edu/icb/icb.do?keyword=k74757&pageid=icb.page414102.

Heine, C., & Quast, H. (2011). Studienentscheidung im Kontext der Studienfinanzierung. Hannover: Hochschulinformationssystem (HIS). Retrieved October 23, 2012, from http://www.dzhw.eu/pdf/pub_fh/fh-201105.pdf.

Henz, U., & Maas, I. (1995). Equal opportunity and educational expansion. *Kölner Zeitschrift für Soziologie und Sozialpsychologie, 47* (4), 605–33.

Hirsch, F. (1977). *Social limits to growth*. London: Routledge & Kegan Paul.

Hopf, W. (2010). *Freiheit – Leistung – Ungleichheit. Bildung und soziale Herkunft in Deutschland*. Weinheim: Juventa.

Hurst, A. (2012). *College and the working class*. Rotterdam: Sense.

Hurst, A.L. (2010). *The burden of academic success*. Lanham; Boulder; New York; Toronto; Plymouth, UK: Lexington Books.

Ingram, N. (2011). Within school and beyond the gate: The complexities of being educationally successful and working class. *Sociology, 45* (2), 287–302.

Institute for Social and Economic Research (ISER) (2013). The European socioeconomic classfication, University of Essex. Retrieved August 12, 2013, from https://www.iser.essex.ac.uk/archives/esec/user-guide/the-european-socio-economic-classification.

Jackson, B., & Marsden, D. (1986). *Education and the working class: Some general themes raised by a study of 88 working-class children in a northern industrial city*. London: Routledge.

Jaroschka, L. (1999) *Abends zur Schule. Zum Stellenwert des Abendgymnasiums im österreichischen Bildungswesen*. Frankfurt am Main: Haag und Herchen.

Jencks, C. (1971). The Coleman Report and the conventional wisdom. In F. Mosteller, & D.P. Moynihan (Eds.) *On equality of educational opportunity* (pp. 69–115). New York: Random House.

Jencks, C., Smith, M., Acland, H., Bane, M.J., Cohen, D., Gintis, H., Heyns, B., and Michelson, S. (1972). *Inequality: A reassessment of the effect of family and schooling in America*. New York: Basic Books.

Kaya, D. (2011). *Die neuen Bildungsaufsteigerinnen. Aufstiegsorientierte Postmigrantinnen in der Einwanderungsgesellschaft*. Marburg: Tectum.

Kepplinger, B. (2000). Aspekte Nationalsozialistischer Herrschaft in Oberösterreich. In E. Tálos, E. Hanisch, W. Neugebauer, & R. Sieder (Eds.) *NS-Herrschaft in Österreich. Ein Handbuch* (pp. 214–36). Wien: öbv.

King, R. (1976). *School and college. Studies of post-sixteen education*, London: Routledge & Kegan Paul.

Kozlik, A. (1965). *Wie wird wer Akademiker? Zum österreichischen Schul- und Hochschulwesen*. Wien: Europa Verlag.

Krais, B. (1989). Soziales Feld, Macht und kulturelle Praxis. Die Untersuchungen Bourdieus über die verschiedenen Funktionen der 'herrschenden Klasse' in Frankreich. In K. Eder (Ed.) *Klassenlage, Lebensstil und kulturelle Praxis. Theoretische und empirische Beiträge zur Auseinandersetzung mit Pierre Bourdieus Klassentheorie* (pp. 47–70). Frankfurt am Main: Surhkamp.

Kröger, M. (2006). *Die Modernisierung der Landwirtschaft. Eine vergleichende Untersuchung der Agrarpolitik in Deutschland und Österreich nach 1945.* Berlin: Logos Verlag.

Langthaler, E. (2000). Eigensinnige Kolonien, NS-Agrarsystem und Bäuerliche Lebenswelten 1938–1945. In E. Tálos, E. Hanisch, W. Neugebauer, & R. Sieder (Eds.) *NS-Herrschaft in Österreich. Ein Handbuch* (pp. 348–75). Wien: öbv.

Lareau, A., & Conley, D. (Eds.) (2008). *Social class: How does it work?* New York: Russell Sage Foundation.

Lehmann, W. (2008). University as vocational education: Working-class students' expectations for university. *British Journal of Sociology of Education, 30,* 137–49.

Lehr, R. (2004). *LandesChronik Oberösterreich.* Wien: Verlag Christian Brandstätter.

Levine, A., & Nidiffer, J. (1996). *Beating the odds: How the poor get to college.* San Francisco: Jossey-Bass.

Lewis, J. (1992). *Women in Britain since 1945. Women, family, work and the state in the post-war years.* Oxford: Blackwell.

Lipset, S.M., & Bendix, R. (1959). *Social mobility in industrial society.* Berkeley: University of California Press.

Lipset, S.M., & Zetterberg, H.L. (1966). A theory of social mobility. In R. Bendix, & S.M. Lipset (Eds.) *Class status and power. Social stratification in comparative perspective* (pp. 561–73). New York: Free Press.

Loew, M. (2013). Das Schulorganisationsgesetz 1962. Retrieved December 31, 2013, from http://austria-forum.org/af/Wissenssammlungen/Essays/Institutionen_Bildung_Kultur/ Das_Schulorganisationsgesetz:1962.

MacArthur, B. (1974). An interim history of the Open University. In J. Tunstall (Ed.) *The Open University opens* (pp. 3–17). London: Routledge & Kegan Paul.

Maguire, M. (2005). Textures of class in the context of schooling: The perceptions of a 'class-crossing' teacher, *Sociology, 39,* 427–43.

Mahony, P., & Zmroczek, C. (1997). Why class matters. In *Class matters: 'Working-class' women's perspectives on social class* (pp. 1–7). London: Taylor & Francis.

McClelland, D.C. (1961). *The achieving society.* Princeton, New Jersey; Toronto London; New York: D. Van Nostrand Company.

McClelland, D.C. (1976). New introduction. In *The achieving society* (pp. A–G). New York et al.: Irvington Publishers.

McIntosh, N. (1974). The OU student. In J. Tunstall (Ed.), *The Open University opens* (pp. 54–65). London: Routledge & Kegan Paul.

Merton, R.K. (1938). Social structure and anomie. *American Sociological Review, 3* (5), 672–82.

Moser, J. (1995). *Oberösterreichische Wirtschaft 1938 bis 1945.* Wien: Böhlau.

Müller, W., & Haun, D. (1994). *Bildungsungleichheit im sozialen Wandel.* Mannheimer Zentrum für Europäische Sozialforschung. Working Papers.

Müller, W., & Karle, W. (1993). *Social selection in educational systems in Europe.* Mannheimer Zentrum für Europäisische Sozialforschung.

Office of Population Census and Surveys (1979). *General household survey 1977.* London: Her Majesty's Stationery Office.

Oldfield, K., & Johnson, R.G. (Eds.) (2008). *Resilience: Queer professors from the working class.* Albany: State University of New York Press.

Ortmann, H. (1971). *Arbeiterfamilie und sozialer Aufstieg. Kritik einer bildungspolitischen Leitvorstellung.* München: Juventa.

Österreichisches Statistisches Zentralamt (1965). *Statistisches Handbuch für die Republik Österreich 1965.* Wien.

Otte, G. (2004). *Sozialstrukturanalysen mit Lebensstilen. Eine Studie zur theoretischen und methodischen Neuorientierung der Lebensstilforschung.* Wiesbaden: Verlag für Sozialwissenschaften.

Pascall, G. (1997). *Social policy. A new feminist analysis.* London and New York: Routledge.

Pateman, C. (1992). The patriarchal welfare state. In L. McDowell, & R. Pringle (Eds.) *Defining women: Social institutions and gender divisions* (pp. 223–45). Cambridge, UK: Polity Press/Open University Press.

Payne, J., Cheng, Y., & Witherspoon, S. (1996). *Education and training for 16–18 year olds in England and Wales. Individual paths and national trends.* London: Policy Studies Institute.

Pilcher, J. (1999). *Women in contemporary Britain. An introduction.* London and New York: Routledge.

Pross, H. (1969). *Über die Bildungschancen von Mädchen in der Bundesrepublik.* Frankfurt am Main: Suhrkamp.

Prümmer, C. (1992). Zur sozialen Herkunft von Fernstudentinnen und Fernstudenten. Fernstudium als Nachholen von Bildungschancen? In A. Schlüter, & B. Borkowski (Eds.) *Arbeitertöchter und ihr sozialer Aufstieg. Zum Verhältnis von Klasse, Geschlecht und sozialer Mobilität* (pp. 173–94). Weinheim: Deutscher Studienverlag.

Reay, D. (1997). The double-bind of the 'working-class' feminist academic: The success of failure or the failure of success? In P. Mahony, & C. Zmroczek (Eds.) *Class matters: 'Working-class' women's perspectives on social class* (pp. 18–29). London: Taylor & Francis.

Reay, D. (2001). Finding or losing yourself? Working-class relationship to education. *Journal of Educational Policy, 16,* 333–46.

Reay, D. (2013). Social mobility, a panacea for austere times: Tales of emperors, frogs and tadpoles, *British Journal of Sociology of Education, 34* (5–6), 660–77.

Reay, D., Crozier, G., & Clayton, J. (2010). 'Fitting in' or 'standing out': Working class students in UK higher education, *British Educational Research Journal, 36* (1), 107–24.

Reay, D., David, M.E., Ball, S., (2005). *Degrees of choice. Social class, race and gender in higher education.* Stoke on Trent: Trentham.

Reay, D., David, M., & Ball, S. (2006). *Degrees of choice. Social class, race and gender in higher education.* Stoke on Trent: Trentham Books.

Rehbein, B., & Saalmann, G. (2003). Feld (*champs*). In G. Fröhlich, & B. Rehbein (Eds.) *Bourdieu-Handbuch Leben-Werk-Wirkung* (pp. 99–103). Stuttgart and Weimar: Verlag J.Betzler.

Reid, W., & Filby, J. (1982). *The Sixth: An essay in education & democracy*. Basingstoke: Falmer Press.

Reinfelder, M. (1997). Switching cultures. In P. Mahony, & C. Zmroczek (Eds.) *Class matters: 'Working-class' women's perspectives on social class* (pp. 101–8). London: Taylor & Francis.

Robbins, D. (1991). *The work of Pierre Bourdieu. Recognizing society*. Buckingham: Open University Press.

Robbins, D. (Ed.) (2000). *Pierre Bourdieu*.4 volumes. London: Sage.

Rohleder, C. (1992). Aus den Sperrsitzen in die höheren Ränge der Gesellschaft? Zum Prozeß der Studienfachwahl von Medizinerinnen aus Arbeiterfamilien und Momenten ihrer aktuellen beruflichen Verortung, in: A. Schlüter (Ed.), *Arbeitertöchter und ihr sozialer Aufstieg. Zum Verhältnis von Klasse, Geschlecht und sozialer Mobilität*. Weinheim: Deutscher Studien Verlag, 124–143.

Rohleder, C. (1997). Aus den Sperrsitzen in die höheren Ränge der Gesellschaft? Zum Prozess der Studienfachwahl von Medizinerinnen aus Arbeiterfamilien und Momenten ihrer aktuellen beruflichen Verortung. In A. Schlüter, & B. Borkoswski (Eds.) *Arbeitertöchter und ihr sozialer Aufstieg. Zum Verhältnis von Klasse, Geschlecht und sozialer Mobilität* (pp. 124–43). Weinheim: Deutscher Studien Verlag.

Rohringer, J. (n.d.). *Zweiter Bildungsweg in Österreich*. Wien: Verlag des österreichischen Gewerkschaftsbundes.

Rosenthal, G. (1993). Reconstruction of life stories: Principles of selection in generating stories for narrative biographical interviews. *The Narrative Study of Lives, Sage, 1* (1), 59–91.

Rosenthal, G. (2004). Biographical research. In C. Seale, G. Gobo, J.F. Gubrium, & D. Silverman (Eds.) *Qualitative Research Practice* (pp. 48–64). London: Sage.

Rosenthal, G. (2008). *Interpretative Sozialforschung. Eine Einführung*. Weinheim and München: Juventa.

Rumble, G. (1982). The Open University of the United Kingdom. An evaluation of an innovative experience in the democratisation of higher education. Open University's Distance Education Research Group Papers 6.

Schaeren, R. (1989). *Das Wirtschaftsgymnasium der Bundesrepublik Deutschland und der Schweiz und die Handelsakademie Österreichs. Ein Vergleich*. Zürich: Rechts- und staatswissenschaftliche Fakultät.

Scheipl, J., & Seel, H. (1988). *Die Entwicklung des österreichischen Schulwesens in der Zweiten Republik 1945–1987*. Graz: Leykam.

Scheipl, J., & Seel, H. (2004). *Das österreichische Bildungswesen am Übergang ins 21. Jahrhundert*. Graz: Leykam.

Schlögl, P. (2007). Von der Lehre zur Hochschule: Möglichkeiten der vertikalen und horizontalen Durchlässigkeit in Österreich. In S. Archan, & P. Schlögl (Eds.) *Von der Lehre zur postsekundären Bildung. Eine Studie und Modelle zur Durchlässigkeit im österreichischen Ausbildungssystem* (pp. 9–25). Wien: Institut für Bildungsforschung der Wirtschaft.

Schlüter, A., & Borkowski, B. (Eds.) (1992). *Arbeitertöchter und ihr sozialer Aufstieg. Zum Verhältnis von Klasse, Geschlecht und sozialer Mobilität*. Weinheim: Deutscher Studienverlag.

Schneeberger, A., & Nowak, S. (2010). *Position der Handelsakademieabsolventen und -absolventinnen im Beschäftigungssystem, ibw-Forschungsbericht Nr. 157*. Wien: Institut für Bildungsforschung der Wirtschaft.

Schools Council Publications (1972). *16–19: Growth and response. 1. Curricular bases*. London: Evans Brothers Limited.

Secondary Heads Association (1979). *On to eighteen. Responses on educational opportunities from 16 to 18*. Basingstoke: Taylor & Francis.

Shavit, Y., & Blossfeld, H.-P. (Eds.) (1993). *Persisting inequality. Changing educational attainment in thirteen countries*. Boulder: Westview Press.

Shavit, Y., Arum, R., & Gamoran, A. (Eds.) (2007). *Stratification in higher education. A comparative study*. Stanford: Stanford University Press.

Simon, B. (1991). *Education and the social order1940–1990*. London: Lawrence & Wishart.

Siraj-Blatchford, I. (2010). Learning in the home and at school: How working class children 'succeed against the odds'. *British Educational Research Journal, 36* (3), 463–82.

Skeggs, B. (1997). Classifying practices: Representations, capitals and recognitions. In P. Mahony, & C. Zmroczek (Eds.) *Class matters: 'Working-class' women's perspectives on social class* (pp. 123–39). London: Taylor & Francis.

Stuart, M. (2012). *Social mobility and higher education. The life experiences of first generation entrants in higher education*. London: Institute of Education Press.

Swartz, D. (1997). *Culture and power. The sociology of Pierre Bourdieu*. Chicago and London: University of Chicago Press.

Tálos, E. (2000). Sozialpolitik in der 'Ostmark'. Angleichungen und Konsequenzen. In E. Tálos, E. Hanisch, W. Neugebauer, & R. Sieder (Eds.) *NS-Herrschaft in Österreich. Ein Handbuch* (pp. 376–408). Wien: öbv.

Tepecik, E. (2011). *Bildungserfolge mit Migrationshintergrund*. Wiesbaden: Verlag für Sozialwissenschaften.

Theling, G. (1986). *Vielleicht wäre ich als Verkäuferin glücklicher geworden. Arbeitertöchter & Hochschule*. Münster: Westfälisches Dampfboot.

Thomas, R. (1974). Admission policy. In J. Tunstall (Ed.) *The Open University opens* (pp. 47–53). London: Routledge & Kegan Paul.

Turner, R.H. (1960). Sponsored and contest mobility and the school system. *American Sociological Review, 25*(6), 855–67.

Turner, R.H. (1964). *The social context of ambition. A study of high-school seniors in Los Angeles*. San Francisco: Chandler Publishing Company.

UNESCO (2013). International Standard Classification of Education (ISCED).

Ungerson, C., & Kember, M. (Eds.) (1997). *Women and social policy. A Reader*, 2nd ed. Houndmills, Basingstoke: Macmillan.

Van Galen, J.A., & Dempsey, V.O. (Eds.) (2009). *The social and educational mobility of education scholars from poor and working class backgrounds*. Rotterdam: Sense Publishers.

Vogl, O. (n.d.). *Die AMS im Spiegel der Zahlen, Schulbericht 1978–1988*.

Weber, M. (1930). *The Protestant ethic and the spirit of capitalism*. London: Allan & Unwin.

Webster, J. (1974). *16–19: The educational explosion*, vol. 1. Exeter: University of Exeter School of Education.

Weis, L. (1990). *Working class without work. High school students in a de-indus-trializing economy.* New York and London: Routledge.

Weischer, C. (2011). *Sozialstrukturanalyse. Grundlagen und Modelle.* Wiesbaden: Verlag für Sozialwissenschaften.

Wengraf, T. (1999). *Biographical methods in social science.* London: Taylor & Francis Group.

Wengraf, T. (2001). *Qualitative research interviewing: Biographic narrative and semi-structured methods.* London: Sense.

Wright, E.O. (Ed.) (2005). *Approaches to class analysis.* Cambridge: Cambridge University Press.

Young, M. (2007). *Bringing knowledge back in. From social constructivism to social realism in the sociology of education.* London: Routledge.

Zinnhobler, R. (2005). *Der lange Weg der Kirche vom Ersten zum Zweiten Vatikanischen Konzil. Beiträge zu Bewegungen und Ereignissen in der katholischen Kirche.* Linz: Verlag Wagner.

Index

Lightning Source UK Ltd.
Milton Keynes UK
UKOW06n2105200415

249989UK00004B/13/P